In "Everyday C ....
his story. I expec. ...., ..., ...y
with many of his joys, frustrations, failures, and victories.
Each vignette is laced with emotion, spiritual insight,
Biblical application, and a smattering of humor. Kent
describes himself as an "ordinary man," without degrees or
position. One should not assume from this that Kent has
nothing to offer to those who seek a deeper walk with the
Lord and a stronger commitment to Biblical values. As I
read Kent's manuscript at 30,000 feet on a cross country
flight, I was challenged, instructed, touched, and moved
and at times would find myself laughing aloud, much to
the amusement of some of my fellow passengers. I encourage you to read and learn from Kent Smith's story. You
may find that, in many respects, it is also your story. You
may also find answers for some of your struggles or at least
the courage to continue the journey.

Truitt Adair, Executive Director
Sunset International Bible Institute
3723 34th Street
Lubbock, Texas

Life is good. Each of us can easily assess how we have
been blessed by God in numerous ways, and thus, we can
boldly exclaim, "Life is really good!" But life is also hard.
Wouldn't you agree? The days of any life are frequently
filled with pain, discomfort, failure, temptation, and sin.

How are we to live in the midst of all of this? Perhaps,
Kent Smith has developed a single set of reminders to
come to the aid of each of us. His work in this book is

motivational, devotional, inspirational, and instructional. With straightforward, real life examples tied to scriptures, Kent reminds us how to live with more joy—even when life is difficult.

Ken Jones
President, Lubbock Christian University

Kent "Grumpy" Smith (even the name of the author hints at self deprecating humor) deftly weaves humor into the fabric of wisdom from the bible and applies it to everyday life in this fine book. It is filled with personal anecdotes that capture your imagination. I felt like a priest at a juicy confession, even though I don't belong to an organized religious denomination…I'm Methodist.

Doc Blakely, Professional Humorist, Wharton, Texas
Dr. James "Doc" Blakely is winner of the National Speakers
Association's highest honors, CSP, CPAE, the Cavett Award, and
one of America's funniest and most entertaining speakers.

Everyday Christianity

TO MY FRIEND JOHN,

TO GOD BE THE GLORY!

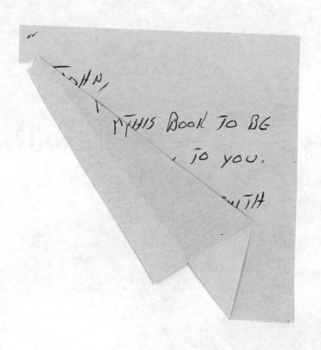

GRUMPY SMITH

Everyday Christianity

LIFE LEARNED LESSONS AND OBSERVATIONS FROM AN **ORDINARY** MAN

TATE PUBLISHING & *Enterprises*

SPECIAL THANKS TO

Steve Stripling, the driving force behind this project. Without you I would have never had the courage to turn my thoughts and feeling into a book. I believe you are the tool God chose to use in getting me to open my eyes to His desire—that I use the gift he blessed me with, the gift of speaking and teaching.

Melissa Baumler, my personal wordsmith. Melissa saw my vision and understood my direction. She took the transcript of my many hours of teaching and placed the words eloquently on paper. I cannot recommend her enough.

www.communique.baumler.net

acknowledgments

There is absolutely no way for me to mention by name everyone I talk about in this book. Space would not allow it. Many of you have had an everlasting impact on my life. Thank you.

Special thanks to my wife, Paula. Having to put up with me for over 31 years must have been a struggle. To Josh and Miranda, I can't believe you would encourage me to write this book. You are, after all, the subject of many of the stories I tell inside.

Thanks to all my family members and brothers and sisters in Christ who supported me with prayers and financing as I worked to get this project published. I couldn't have done it without you.

Finally, to my parents Homer and Glenda Smith. It is only through my experience as a parent and grandparent that I am coming to fully understand your love for me. Thanks for all the love you have given me. Thanks for teaching me to respect others, work hard, love much and serve God.

God, I'm sorry it has taken me almost 52 years to begin fully using the gift You gave me—the gift of speaking and teaching. Now that I have opened my heart to Your will, please use me as You see fit. I know that with You at the controls, this ministry will be blessed, lives will be changed, and souls will be saved.

Father, it is my prayer that You bless this book, my writing and my speaking ministry. I am, after all, an ordinary man trying to live Christianity every day. I can't accomplish this alone; I have to have You beside me.

TABLE OF CONTENTS

INTRODUCTION

Have you ever had the burning need to tell people how you feel? Have you ever felt led to open your heart and lay all your inner thoughts on the table for everyone to see, knowing all the while that what they discover may not be pretty? I have felt that burning deep inside me, and I believe that feeling came from God.

My ideas for sharing what was on my heart were so different, and the style so unusual, that I went to the elders of my local church to ask if I could present my experiences as a series of Bible classes. My lesson each week would involve singing and props. The class would incorporate some of my personal stories and jaw-dropping confessions. Songs would include, not only traditional church songs, but also pop and rock songs that expressed the messages I needed to convey.

Over the next 14 weeks, I opened my heart as never before. The Kent Smith God knew was now being introduced fully to my Christian brothers and sisters. There were moments of laughter and times when one class member would poke another. Periods of uncontrolled tears were followed a few minutes later by looks of, "I can't believe he just said that."

The result was that God used me to touch the lives of those who listened. Everyone, it seemed, could identify with me. Many had been where I had been. Others were experiencing challenges in their lives they could not handle, and now they were seeing that they were not alone. My failures helped them to overcome their failures. My stories and experiences of love and service helped them to better appreciate the love and success in their lives.

I think the reason why so many were touched is simply because I am just an ordinary man. I am not a minister, and I don't have a PhD. I don't have a single hour of higher education. All I had to offer was a life exposed for all to see. Much of it was not pretty, some of it was fun, and most of it was interesting, but my brothers and sisters could identify with it. After all, when the pretense is gone and the microscope applied, we are all just ordinary people trying to live out Christianity every day.

That brings us to this book. A few months ago, Steve Stripling, a dear brother, was talking to me after a Sunday morning Bible class on the Gospel of John. When he mentioned he was struggling with a certain issue, I told him I had addressed that topic in a series I taught a couple of years ago titled *Everyday Christianity: Life-Learned Lessons and Observations from an Ordinary Man.* I told him the lessons were on CD and offered him a copy.

Steve listened to the entire series in about two weeks, and when he had finished, he told me I had to write a book. When I told him that I am not a writer, he really opened my eyes by saying, "Kent, the book is already written. All you have to do is put on paper what you said in your recorded lessons!"

So, my friends, what you hold in your hands are the stories of an ordinary man who opened his heart and allowed God to use him in a way he never dreamed possible. It is my prayer that by reading this book, you will be touched in the ways you need to be touched. To Him be the glory.

one
Be Still

Be still! If I've heard it once, I've heard it a hundred times. My freshman science teacher, Mr. Baker, used to say it all the time. I didn't understand what he meant back then. The important thing is…I understand it now.

If you are like me, you feel that if you were to slow down right now, you'd get run over by someone or something. Actually, I often feel that if I were to slow down and be still, I'd get run over by life! Sometimes, I have so many irons in the fire I don't know if I'm pick'n up the iron in my hand or putt'n it down.

When I was twenty, I thought I would have it made by now and life would be going at a nice, slow pace. Now that I'm almost fifty, I realize life may never slow down. When our two children were babies, they kept my wife, Paula, and me running all the time, and we loved it. Once they started school, things really heated up. Both kids were involved in a lot of activities and there were always contests, plays or events to attend.

School was a top priority to us, and we expected the children to do the best they could. Going to church was also important to us as a family. If the doors were open, we were there. There were always a lot of social activities at church and we felt it was very important that we be a part of those activities. Another thing that kept us running was sports. Both Josh and Miranda were active in sports, and since I lived vicariously through my kids, I was not about to let one sporting opportunity go by.

I haven't even mentioned our jobs yet. Paula and I both worked and, fortunately, we had jobs that allowed us a lot of freedom and flexibility. This enabled us to be involved in our children's activities, go to church, and have a good social life.

I'm going to brag on Paula, so listen up. When Paula and I decided to get married, she had attended one year of college. Like many twenty-year-olds, who think they have all the answers, we decided she didn't need to continue her education, so she quit. After Miranda, our youngest, started kindergarten, Paula decided to go back to college. She was still working a part-time job and, if that wasn't enough, we lived in the country, so she had to drive seventy-five miles each way to attend Texas Tech. Yet even with her busy schedule, our quality of life never changed.

There is no doubt in my mind that Paula is the reason why our family has succeeded and been so close for twenty-nine years. She has juggled an amazing amount of work and activities during all this time. Despite her many roles as wife, mother, employee, student, and everyday Christian, she has always been there for our children and me.

I could tell other stories, but I think you understand where I'm coming from. No matter how old you are, life keeps you busy. I think it is part of Satan's plan. He wants us to be so busy and so overwhelmed that we forget God, our families, and our commitment to service.

DON'T LET LIFE PASS BY

We are all so busy that we sometimes need to slow down—
and even stop—we need to just be still. We need to take
the time to really enjoy God. We must savor every minute
we have as a married couple joined together by God. We
need to be still even though we are busy in order to enjoy
the full impact of the children God has given us.

There's a song by Jim Croce that relates to this thought.
One of the phrases in the song is "…moving ahead so life
won't pass me by." I have come to look at this in a different way: "Slow down and don't pass life by" (I'll tell some
stories later that will help me drive home this point and
help you realize what you might be missing when you run
too fast).

The country group Alabama sings a song with a line
that says, "All I really gotta do is live and die, but I'm in
a hurry and don't know why." Now those, my friends, are
words to ponder. You and I need to learn that all that's
certain in life is living and dying. It's up to us to decide
how we do both. We determine what we will leave behind
and where we will be after our earthly lives are over.

One song we sing in church is "Be Still and Know." The
songwriter is anonymous, but the inspiration comes from
Psalm 46:10. Three times in verse one, the writer tells us to
"be still and know." Those are words to live by. Let them
soak in. Be still long enough to close your eyes and hear
the song. Let it reveal the peace in knowing and believing
that God gives you strength.

I want to share a few more verses from Psalm 46, starting at verse 1 and continuing through verse 11:

God is our refuge and strength, an ever-present help in trouble. Therefore we will not fear, though the earth give way and the mountains fall into the heart of the sea, though its waters roar and foam and the mountains quake with their surging. There is a river whose streams make glad the city of God, the holy place where the Most High dwells. God is within her, she will not fall; God will help her at break of day. Nations are in uproar, kingdoms fall; he lifts his voice, the earth melts. The LORD Almighty is with us; the God of Jacob is our fortress. Come and see the works of the LORD, the desolations he has brought on the earth. He makes wars cease to the ends of the earth; he breaks the bow and shatters the spear, he burns the shields with fire. "Be still, and know that I am God; I will be exalted among the nations, I will be exalted in the earth." The LORD Almighty is with us; the God of Jacob is our fortress.

Let's make this personal, folks. If you are in God, God is in you. When you are in trouble, God is your refuge and strength. You do not need to be afraid when it seems everything around you is falling apart. When everything is crumbling and you don't think there is hope for taking another step, the Lord Almighty is with you. God has power over all things, and, friends, that includes you! All you have to do is "Be still, and know that I am God" (v. 10).

I believe there are three areas in our lives that need to be stilled: (1) our bodies, (2) our mouths and (3) our minds.

STILLING OUR BODIES

First of all, I'm convinced that we need to learn to physically slow down and be still. Have you ever noticed how much noise is generated by a group of people without anyone saying a word? I was talking to my friend, Brad Smith, about this the other day. Brad is a band teacher in one of our local middle schools. He said, "It's unbelievable, just the commotion and the noise that fifty kids can make even when they're not talking. Just the movement is noise." We're not necessarily talking about the volume of the noise; it's just the commotion. Commotion can be distracting, and when we let ourselves be distracted, we can pass right by life.

Let's say you are a parent and the time is nearing for your firstborn to take his or her first step. Your baby is hanging on to the table and just about to let go when, all of a sudden, the doggie door swings open and you turn away because of the commotion. Your baby takes the first step and then the second, and just as you look back at your bundle of joy, you see him or her fall. It won't be the last step your infant ever takes, but noise, clutter, and busyness made you look away long enough to miss that first step. This time, it was a milestone you missed. The next time you turn around, you might realize your baby is leaving for college and you've missed those critical years to enjoy and influence that child.

At the beginning of the chapter, I mentioned I had a science teacher named Mr. Baker who would tell us to be still. His class would consist of him just picking up his science book and reading it aloud to the students. Can you picture a class of high school freshmen actually listening? It's not that we were talking, but we were always moving around. I learned one day that you can take a surgical hose, put it on the end of one of those high-pressure nozzles you find in any science lab, and shoot water twenty-five to thirty feet. You can soak somebody down pretty quickly—and you can do it while your teacher is reading a book aloud to the class.

Every now and then, Mr. Baker would look up and shout, "Be still!" I didn't understand what he meant by that at the time. Didn't he mean for us to be quiet? I know what he means now. Be still and listen. Be still and understand what's going on around you. Physically be still. It doesn't take a lot of movement to make a lot of noise.

How do you feel when you're talking to a friend and he or she is fidgeting? You're pouring your heart out, but all you see is fidgeting. Is the person listening? No. Be still and know. Acknowledge other people when they are talking to you. Give them the respect they deserve.

Psalm 46 tells us to be still and know. I believe Jesus teaches the same lesson in the book of Revelation. Jesus identifies Himself to John in Revelation 1:17–18:

"...Do not be afraid. I am the First and the Last.

I am the Living One; I was dead, and behold I am alive for ever and ever! And I hold the keys of death and Hades.

After His introduction, Jesus tells John to write to the seven churches. Toward the end of each letter, Jesus says, "He who has an ear, let him hear what the Spirit says to the churches" (Rev. 2:7, 11, 17, 29; 3:6, 13, 22).

What point do you think Jesus is trying to make? I think the point is that we should act on what we hear. I believe He is telling us to be still and pay attention, because what He has said is a matter of life and death. It's a matter of enjoying what He has given us. A matter of being the kind of Christian, mom, dad, brother, sister, employee, boss, or anyone else He would have us be.

STILLING OUR MOUTHS

Secondly, we need to learn to be quiet. In other words, shut up! We need to be quiet and listen to those around us. Many of us need to set our ego aside and realize it's not about us. When other people are talking, we need to listen to what they're saying and not think about how we're going to rebut. We need to stop thinking about how we're going to tell about our grandkids as soon as they take a breath while talking about theirs. (Wow, I just stepped on my own toes!) Remember, other people have a life too, and they want to tell us about it. When we're too busy talking or thinking about what we're going to say next, we don't hear what others are saying.

God has tremendous patience with us. How many

times have we been busy talking when He is talking? This problem all started in the Garden of Eden with God's most prized creation. In Genesis 3:9–13, Adam answers a question from God that God already knows the answer to:

> But the LORD God called to the man, "Where are you?" He answered, "I heard you in the garden, and I was afraid because I was naked; so I hid." And he said, "Who told you that you were naked? Have you eaten from the tree that I commanded you not to eat from?" The man said, "The woman you put here with me—she gave me some fruit from the tree, and I ate it." Then the LORD God said to the woman, "What is this you have done?" The woman said, "The serpent deceived me, and I ate."

Do you see what's going on here? Adam and Eve are too busy, too curious, and too much like us to listen when God tells them not to eat of the fruit of the tree of the knowledge of good and evil. Then, just like you and I, they began to talk. God already knows what happened, but Adam and Eve start justifying themselves and, in doing so, lay the blame on someone or something else. If only they had listened. If only they had made up their minds to be still when God spoke the first time.

STILLING OUR MINDS

Thirdly, we need to learn how to keep our minds still. When it comes down to it, isn't that really the most important thing we need to control? After all, the mind controls everything that is physical in us. It has the ability to stop the fidgeting and the tongue.

Throughout the remainder of this book, I am going to open my heart and life to you. I confess that most of what you will read is an indictment of my weaknesses. I am sharing these faults in hopes that you will be strengthened when you find yourself in a similar situation.

I'm going to tell you a short story about stilling the mind. Once, when I was going through a difficult time, I went to see an elder in our church named Vance Bryan at his home. I went to him for counsel because he is a wonderfully caring person and possibly the least judgmental person I know. Having said that, I'll now say that Vance is slanted a little differently than me. You see, Vance is a "glass half full" kind of guy, where as I'm a "glass is almost empty" fella. Vance is big into the "be still" concept while I am more of the "hurry up and get done so I can worry about something else" type person. He lives out the motto, "Stop and smell the roses." Me? I say, "I don't see any stink'n roses."

We talked for a while, and then Vance said, "Let's go outside." The next thing I knew, I was sitting on the grass in his backyard with my rear on the ground and my legs crossed in front of me. I thought, *Man, this hurts.* Then Vance said, "Look at this flower; take in the beauty of the petals." Folks, most of my life has been spent on a farm in west Texas, so as I sat there with my knees aching and back cramping and rear growing numb from sitting on the ground, all I could see was something that looked like a weed. Back home, we would have been hoeing that thing!

From this experience, I learned that I needed to keep my mind quiet. I discovered that I needed to look for the beauty in God's creation and stop passing judgments based on past experiences. Vance chose to see the beauty with a quiet mind while I chose to see a problem that never existed.

WAYS TO ENJOY A PEACEFUL LIFE

So what are some practical things we can do to enjoy a long, quiet, and peaceful life? Here are three suggestions I've learned along the way.

Don't Worry

I am beginning to realize that worry is extremely unproductive and cumbersome. Just think about all the weight worry puts on your shoulders. Let's look at what the writer of Psalm 37:1–9 said.

> Do not fret because of evil men or be envious of those who do wrong; for like the grass they will soon wither, like green plants they will soon die away. Trust in the LORD and do good; dwell in the land and enjoy safe pasture. Delight yourself in the LORD and he will give you the desires of your heart. Commit your way to the LORD; trust in him and he will do this: He will make your righteousness shine like the dawn, the justice of your cause like the noonday sun. Be still before the LORD and wait patiently for him; do not fret when men succeed

in their ways, when they carry out their wicked schemes. Refrain from anger and turn from wrath; do not fret—it leads only to evil. For evil men will be cut off, but those who hope in the LORD will inherit the land.

In this passage, God is telling us not to worry. He has everything under control. (I'm talking to myself as much as I am to you when I say that this concept needs to be applied to our lives.) How much time have we all spent worrying about things or even about what we're going to worry about next? The stress we put on ourselves because we don't turn things over to God is unbelievable. We don't share our burdens with each other. We tell ourselves, *I'm just going to handle this myself.* I've been to some pretty low places during the last few years, but I've always felt better after I talked to dear friends like Vance Bryan, and Tim Pyles my minister. These are godly men whom I hold dear. I look up to them, I esteem these guys, and I am blessed that they are willing to listen.

Don't Be Afraid

Most of the things we fear never happen anyway. Let's look at Exodus 14:13–14:

Moses answered the people, "Do not be afraid. Stand firm and you will see the deliverance the LORD will bring you today. The Egyptians you see today you will never see again. The LORD will fight for you; you need only to be still."

Moses speaks these words to the Israelites as they're looking over their shoulders to see the Egyptian army with chariots and horses bearing down on them. They're hemmed in with the desert on one side and the sea on the other. Man, talk about fear! Can you relate? Sounds like our lives sometimes, doesn't it? It's unbelievable the pain that fear causes us. But Moses tells the people that the Lord will fight for them. All they have to do is be still.

So how does this story end? Well, the Lord parts the Red Sea, giving the Israelites an escape route right through the middle on dry land. The Egyptians pursue them, but they aren't so lucky. The waters of the sea are released and the entire Egyptian army is drowned. The Israelites have just witnessed the awesome power of the Lord. Don't forget that God does the same for us. He provides us with safe passage and protection when we simply still our souls, put aside our fear and trust in Him.

One of the most common fears in America is the fear of rejection. People thrive on acceptance. We do our best to be appreciated and acknowledged. We need to know that other people love us. Rejection wounds. It has the ability to injure a person of confidence, and destroy a person of low self-esteem. I hate rejection! I don't ask for business because I don't want people to tell me no. I used to spend hours building up the courage to ask a girl for a date. There has only been one girl in my life that was given the privilege of turning me down twice. I don't know how I ever convinced myself to walk up to her at a football game and ask her out…again. She had already rejected me once, and that was usually my limit.

You may be wondering about now how I ended up married. Well, it wasn't because Paula never turned me down for a date. I never gave her the chance to turn me down because I never "officially" asked her out. I just made sure I was always where she was. We went to the same church and attended the same young adult Bible class. I always made sure that we just happened to sit next to one another. Then when church or class was over and the group went out to eat or to a devotional I would be right there beside her. Finally after a few times of being in the same place all the time I walked her to her car one night in the church parking lot. We had never had a "date," but I felt like maybe, (if God was on my side) if I did ask her for a date she would most likely say yes. So there I was about to ask her out when she stepped toward me and kissed me…on the lips!

I did what any self respecting, red-blooded American young man would do. I told her good night and opened the car door for her. After that I figured, why ask her out when things are working out pretty well as they are. It was a not long after that that I knew I wanted to marry Paula. The thing was, how could I ask her to marry me? I mean, if she were to turn me down I wouldn't be able to live with myself. So one night a group of us were studying for an exam. We were in the Sunset Church of Christ building in Lubbock, Texas. I was enrolled in the Adventures In Missions program that the Sunset School of Preaching offers for single college age adults. Paula was not with us. She was upstairs in a teacher's workroom getting material ready for a kid's class she was teaching on Sunday. I had finally gotten my courage up. I had abscessed four teeth by gritting them together while working up the guts, but now was the time. I went upstairs in the church building and ask her if she would go to Grand Junction, Colorado with me "as one" to work as a youth minister there. And she said yes!

Be Open to the Ideas of Others

When you listen, you hear ideas different from your own. It's difficult to learn something when you're always talking. Here's the thing, if I am always listening to me, what can I learn? I mean, let's face it I already know what I'm telling myself. The reality is that once I convince myself that I am absolutely right I instantly reject anyone who has a different opinion. So, the lesson for me is this, I need to have my mouth and ears beaten to a pulp with a good case of humility. Now that is a simple, yet difficult concept. I have to realize, humbling myself before God also means being humble before men. I know I tend not to listen to people when I think I'm smarter than they are. Humility takes care of that weakness.

Listen. Be still. Pay attention. Understand. In Mark 4:37–40, Jesus illustrates the point of listening beautifully:

> A furious squall came up, and the waves broke over the boat, so that it was nearly swamped. Jesus was in the stern, sleeping on a cushion. The disciples woke him and said to him, "Teacher, don't you care if we drown?" He got up, rebuked the wind and said to the waves, "Quiet! Be still!" Then the wind died

down and it was completely calm. He said to his disciples, "Why are you so afraid? Do you still have no faith?"

Jesus had been teaching these men. They had walked with Him and been with Him every day. They had seen Him perform miracles, and yet when they felt their lives were in danger, they forgot about everything He had taught them. Jesus said, "Why do you have fear? Haven't you been listening?" That's what He's asking, really: Haven't you been listening? Do you still have no faith? After all, if they had been still—if they had been listening, if they had been paying attention—they would have understood that they weren't going to drown because the Son of Man was in the boat with them.

Remember the story in Matthew 14 about Jesus walking on the water and Peter wanting to join him? Peter "listened" for a moment when he stepped out on the water. Then he became distracted. He wasn't still, he wasn't focused, and he didn't concentrate on the Lord. And, as a result, he started to sink.

LOOK FOR THE SPECIAL MOMENTS

We can all look back on special memories when we wish we had been still. I recently sat down to make a list of such times in my life. I was glad to see that the list wasn't too long, but it reminded me of the moments when I let other concerns get in the way of embracing the simple things in life. Here are some of the times I wished I'd been still:

1. I like a lot of ice in whatever I'm drinking. Whatever drink I have, I want to start with a glass full of ice and then pour the drink over it. Some folks say, "You don't get as much that way." That's all right; I'm enjoying what I have. Well, we had some plastic ice cubes in the shape of fish and seashells in the freezer, and when I came home one day, Miranda brought me a Coke to drink. She used the plastic ice cubes instead of regular ice. You know what? I wasn't still. I didn't enjoy the moment because those plastic cubes weren't like real ice. I didn't show her the courtesy she deserved. I should have focused on sitting down and making that the best Coke I ever had in my life because my daughter had prepared it with love just for me. I wish I had done that.

2. I previously mentioned that my wife, Paula, attended Texas Tech, which was seventy-five miles away from where we lived. One time, the car had problems, so I needed to change the transmission filter. I am no mechanic. I hate mechanical work. When I use wrenches, I end up with skinned knuckles, which makes me angry. It's just one of those short-fuse things. Anyway, I had to do this job, so I jacked up the car. My son, Josh, who was probably eight years old at the time, was there with me and was helping me by handing me the wrench. I twisted the wrench and promptly busted my knuckle. When I finally got the pan off, I ended up with transmission fluid all over me. I was not enjoying the project at all. And there was Josh. He was

there just helping me. We finished, and I cleaned up. Josh went into the house and said, "Mom, this is the best day of my life." You know why? He was with his dad. He enjoyed that time. And what was I doing? I was saying, "Give me that stinking wrench. I have to get this job done so I can move on to something else." I didn't slow down and enjoy the moment.

3. We had a summer recreation program for children in Denver City, Texas, where we raised our kids. There were track meets and other activities for which the children could win ribbons. It was a big deal, and all the kids in town participated. I think Miranda was running the hundred-yard dash. She was a little bitty thing with a frizzy perm and glasses twice the size of her face. She was running along and could have won the race, except for the fact that she was with her best friend and just skipping along and smiling at her. I was in the stands going bonkers, screaming, "Run! Run! You have to win!" Miranda was just having fun. Be still and enjoy those moments. Be still and enjoy life.

4. There's nothing more precious than those quiet times you spend reading to your children and letting them read to you. I wish I had spent more time with my kids in my lap, just reading to them.

5. My son, Josh, is a better dad than I ever thought of being because he takes the time to lie down with his kids. He is also patient when he instructs them. He talks to his daughter, Mary Alice, and explains to her

why she shouldn't do this or that. I didn't have time for that. I just yanked Josh up, gave him three swats with my belt or whatever was close and thought I was being an effective parent. The patience I see in Josh now amazes me. I wonder where in the world it came from. I wish I had been more like Josh when I was raising him and Miranda.

6. Josh and I went to Dallas once when he was a freshman or sophomore in high school. We made it a father/son sports trip to watch Mavericks and Cowboys games. Both teams lost terribly, but it was still a great time because we shared those experiences. I wish I had been still often enough to take more father/son trips. Make it a priority to spend quality time with your children.

7. Miranda had jobs and made her own money, but she always expressed interest in working with me on the farm. "Dad," she would say, "I'll work on the farm." I always just sloughed it off. I spent several years with Josh on the farm, and he spent several years with his granddad on the farm. The relationships we developed were amazing. I wish I had been still and taken Miranda up on her offer, because time slips by so quickly. Don't let this happen to you.

AVOID MISSED MEMORIES

To help you keep from having a long list of missed memories, I want to share a few important points for you to keep in mind. If you remember and embrace these blessings, I think you will live a richer life.

1. *Know you're loved.* I believe love is the most powerful force in the world. It makes us do things we never thought we could do. People give up their lives for love. Being loved is one of the greatest motivators in the world.

2. *Laugh so hard your face hurts.* I don't know if I've ever done that, but I've laughed so hard that my stomach hurt for a week. The unfortunate thing is I haven't done it in about twenty years.

3. *See your own features reflected in your children's faces.* When Major, my grandson, was born, we spent four months and three weeks saying, "Who does he look like?" We finally decided he didn't look like anyone. He just looked like Major.

   One night around that time, I was holding Major and he was leaning backward over the chair as I was tickling him. Just as he lifted his head up, I saw my younger self reflected in his face. I said, "That is my one-year-old birthday picture." Oh, man, it was unbelievable. I didn't say a word to the family, because I didn't want them groaning and rolling their eyes. (Well, actually, I figure it's a bad deal if the kid looks like me. He's going to be beating women off for the rest of his life. It's a terrible curse.)

   We went to a share group meal that same evening at the church building. It had only been fifteen or twenty minutes since I noticed the resemblance. When I walked in with Major in my arms, one of our friends looked at us from across the kitchen and said, "Oh, my goodness, Kent, That little boy looks just like you." I said, "Yes, I saw that five minutes ago." Five minutes later, some other friends walked in. They had never seen our grandson before. They looked at me holding him and said, "He looks just like you."

Take time to notice those special moments. Savor the resemblance and exhibit a life worthy of reflection. You have more influence over your children and grandchildren than you may realize. They will always be watching you and picking up your mannerisms, so make sure your life leaves the kind of impression you would want to see reflected in them.

4. *Laugh at yourself.* A good friend of mine says, "Never wander too far from your own laughter." Take the time to laugh at yourself. Most of my life, I've been too busy proving myself. As a result, I've taken myself too seriously. I've lived life as if I were in a constant state of constipation, so uptight about making a mistake that I couldn't even breathe.

5. *Hold hands with someone you love.* I will talk about the importance of touch in another chapter, so for now just consider how you felt the first time you held hands with someone special. I remember my first date with my first real girlfriend. I was driving back to her house, and she was sitting next me, and about two miles before I got her home The Beatles came on the radio singing, "I

want to hold your hand." I started singing with them. It was my way of asking if I could hold her hand. The dumb thing is I still didn't reach out and take her hand. I think fear crept in and set up a roadblock in my mind. I completely forgot that she was sitting right next to me, and I never thought she might want to hold hands, too. I just figured I was lucky to have her go out with me in the first place. I remember how special I felt once I did take her hand. Not only did she not slap my face, she actually held on tight.

6. *Have someone tell you that you're beautiful.* How do you feel when someone compliments you? We all enjoy being told we are beautiful or handsome. You can take this concept beyond a person's physical appearance as well. You should never be shy about complimenting others on their great qualities or a job well done because people thrive on admiration and pats on the back. When you compliment others in this manner, you can see the effect in their smile, and when you see their smile, you smile! Wow, a better life for all of us.

7. *Be thankful for your friends.* One of my favorite movies is *Tombstone*. In this great western, Doc Holliday is going to fight a battle he really shouldn't be fighting, and one of the other cowboys asks Doc why he's there. He doesn't think Doc has a stake in the fight. Doc tells him that Wyatt Earp is his friend, and that is why he is there. The cowboy says that he himself has a lot of friends, questioning why Doc would put his life in danger for one friend. Doc simply lets the man know

that he doesn't have a lot of friends, and the point is made. Doc may not have many friends, but he is willing to die for the one friend he does have. Be thankful for your friends.

8. *Cherish your first kiss.* Oh man, I broke the steering wheel on my Chevy Malibu after my first kiss. Unbelievable! Those things used to be plastic—not like they're made now. I got back in the car after kissing this girl goodnight, and I hit the steering wheel hard and let out a scream. I'm not sure whether it was the hit or the scream, but it broke.

So the message is simple: Be still. Take the time to enjoy life. Embrace the tender moments of your relationships. Soak in the wonder of your children. Absorb God's glory. Rest in His comfort.

I have a scar on my right elbow from trying to outrun Josh when he was about twelve years old. My body got ahead of my legs, and down I went. The track I fell on scraped the skin right off of my elbow. It wasn't a serious wound, but I still have a visible reminder of what can happen when I try to run faster than my capabilities.

When I try to outrun life and end up falling, I risk more serious damage than a minor physical scar. It can mean missing a precious first step or the chance of a lifetime trip, even if the trip is an impromptu father-daughter breakfast at McDonald's.

Be still and know…

emotion of DeVOTION
TWO

What turns your crank? What gets you excited? What makes you stand up and pay attention? We live our lives with either joy or dread depending on the emotions we have for the people and events we encounter. We can choose to put forth little or no effort and muddle through our responsibilities and encounters with people, or, if we have a vested interest in people and activities, we can choose to be actively involved in other people's lives.

In other words, we can simply cope with people or we can choose to become involved with people. We can just endure our work, or we can love what we do for a living. One spouse may love the arts, while the other spouse tolerates them. One person can't get enough of sports, while the other person puts up with hours of televised games for the sake of his or her spouse; even though he or she thinks watching sports is a waste of time.

The same idea holds true in our worship to God. One person longs to go to worship, while another goes only out of obligation. One serves the Father with great love and passion, while the other serves out of fear. One becomes involved in service to God and others, while another enters worship late, leaves before the last prayer, and has no thought of serving others.

One aspect of worship that has come to the forefront

during the last couple of decades is worship style. Some churches have begun to use musical instruments in worship. Those who once used only a piano now have full bands. One group continues to have one song leader; another has a praise team. One congregation may clap and raise hands; another practices a more conservative worship style. Preferences and the desire to meet the needs of the congregation and community often drive decisions as to what style of worship will be adopted.

My intention is not to defend or attack any of the styles mentioned above. Instead, I want to examine the motivations behind our worship and service. Ultimately, the questions are: What do we bring to the table? How and why do we choose to be involved in worship and service to God? Is our relationship with the Father one-sided, with Him always giving and us always receiving? Do we attend worship or serve on a committee out of obligation and to get another star by our name in the church directory? Or do we invest ourselves in the work and worship of God to His glory and honor, no matter the cost?

THE TWO SIDES OF EMOTION

If you look up the word "emotion" in *Webster's New Dictionary* 1998 *edition,* you will find it defined as "mental agitation" or "an excited state of feeling." I was surprised by the first definition because "mental agitation" carries a negative meaning to me. Strangely enough, I generally look at the downside of every situation first—you know, what could go wrong instead of what could go right. However,

I wasn't surprised by the definition of "an excited state of feeling." Once I took time to think about it, I realized that an excited state could be positive or negative.

Some questions to ask ourselves on a deeply personal level are: How emotional are we in terms of our devotion to God? What form of emotion do we bring to worship and service? Those of you who know me would describe me as an emotional person. I cry at the drop of a hat. Tears seem to come out of nowhere. One sister in our congregation said her husband once used me as an example of how often she cries. The comment? "You cry as much as Kent Smith does!" Wow, I never knew I had that kind of reputation.

It's true. I do cry a lot in worship. I can be right in the middle of a Bible verse or the chorus of a hymn and just break out in tears. Sometimes it's brought on by the realization of my unworthiness; other times, I cry just listening to the words of a song. I become emotionally involved in a heart-changing way. I have also had times of mental agitation during worship. They occur when I allow negative feelings about someone to invade my mind or when I make judgments as to the way certain things should be done.

The nature of humans is to be right and to win. I like to have things the way I want them, no matter how others feel. When I find myself mentally agitated, it is usually because things are not being done the way I think they should be done or because I have feelings I should not have against someone.

For those of you who have never attended one of my classes, I almost always speak and teach to myself. In fact,

I have bloodied my toes many times by stomping on them. I don't want you to be offended by anything I write in this book; however, if your toes do get stepped on, take a moment to consider why. If your feet are hurting because of truth, move your feet to a lighted path and walk as God would have you walk.

As we begin to look at our emotion of devotion, let me offer a few stories to help illustrate the point. Some folks become emotionally involved when watching the players on the field during high school football games. Others get goose bumps watching the marching bands during half-time. Dale Boulter, a good friend of mine, told me once that football was invented so the band would have a place to perform. Now, I ask you, how ridiculous is that?

It's not hard to figure out that his son was the drum major and my son was the quarterback. Both Dale and I were invested in the game, but each had a different take on which activity was the most important. Dale was more critical (mental agitation) of a misstep of a marcher or the sound of a stray note, but I was upset (mental agitation) by the breakdown of a lineman who allowed my son to be flattened. Dale had an excited state of feeling over a flawless halftime show. I felt the same way about the game itself and wanted the band to get out of the way so the game could resume.

Dale would sit and watch the game in anticipation of halftime. I would sit and watch the halftime show think-ing about the second half of the game. There was another group of folks I haven't mentioned yet. They were the ones who only sat through the event that interested them. Some left for refreshments at halftime, while others came to sit in the stands just for halftime. Which are you in terms of church and worship? Do you disengage in some areas and become involved in others? Are you critical of the minister and wish he would wrap up his message so the music could start again?

So, back to high school football. The summer before Josh's junior year, I was a football official in our hometown of Denver City, Texas. Josh was working to win the starting position as strong safety on our football team, the Denver City Mustangs. Every August as two-a-day practices came to an end and the football season approached, high school football teams would have scrimmages against each other. It was during these scrimmages that teams and officials got tuned up for the season.

The teams from opposing schools would meet head to head to run their best offense and defense against one another. This was the first time each year the players got to hit someone other than their own teammates. The fans rarely knew what was going on, because each team had a set number of plays that their offense would run. Scores didn't matter (yeah, right), and the time was used to fine-tune the offense and defense for the season. The team of officials honed their skills as well. And though there were 11 players from each team active for any given play, there were always extra players on the field, along with several coaches and referees.

I was on the field when Josh proved himself as a strong safety. The quarterback from the opposing team had a reputation for being a great athlete among the small schools from the area. He was the main man for his team, and any coach from any level of high school football would have picked him for their team in a heartbeat. As one of the plays started to develop, I was in position as the back judge of a five-man officiating crew and was able to view the entire field from behind the defense. The play flowed to my right, and I will admit to all you referees out there that I was not taking care of my job because Josh was on the field in the position of strong safety. I saw the quarterback I just told you about take the ball and move to his left. He saw the hole and chose to keep the ball and turn up the field. At that very moment, I saw Josh fill the gap the quarterback had seen. The two players collided. The hit was massive. Both players unloaded all they had, and both held their ground. The quarterback advanced no further, and Josh did not push him back. The play ended with both on the ground. Josh had held his own. Chills went up and down my spine as the defensive back coach began yelling Josh's name and jumping up and down in celebration of a job well done.

It would have been inappropriate for me to hug Josh at that moment, but I sure wanted to. I was emotionally involved. I had an excited state of feeling. I felt privileged to be there and was so proud as I witnessed the accomplishment of one of my children up close and personal.

God knows that feeling. He has been on the field with me as I served Him. He has been on the field with you as well. He has seen you hold your ground when you met the opposition. He has heard the accolades you received from fellow Christians for a job done well. He has felt the goose bumps run up His spiritual spine as you stood your ground against the enemy. He has wanted to take you under His wing and wrap you in His love. I'm reminded of Matthew 3:16–17. This short passage gives us a glimpse of the love God has for His Son:

> As soon as Jesus was baptized, he went up out of the water. At that moment heaven was opened, and he saw the Spirit of God descending like a dove and lighting on him. And a voice from heaven said, "This is my Son, whom I love; with him I am well pleased."

Now I know how God felt as he proclaimed his feelings for his Son. The Father affirmed Jesus, just as I have affirmed that Josh is my son many times. The amazing thing is that God has affirmed you and me, too. If you have obeyed Him, you have been affirmed.

EMOTION IN WORSHIP

So what kind of emotion do you bring to the table in terms of worship? How excited are you to go to worship? Are you there to be entertained? Are you there to perform? Are you there to see and be seen? Do you do the "church thing" because you are expected to or are required to be there? Are you there to worship the God of heaven with all your heart? The answer to these questions may give you insight into the kind of emotion you feel during worship. Are you agitated or excited?

Let's go back to football for a minute. I want to move

from the scrimmage I told you about to the first game of the season. Josh didn't start the game at strong safety as he had hoped. However, around the third defensive stand, Josh found out he would be entering the game. I received another privilege to be a part of the game—this time not as a game official but as a radio color commentator. The local radio station aired all of the football and basketball games. I was not normally part of the broadcast, but one of the announcers was sick that night, so they called and asked me to fill in. I jumped at the opportunity.

On the night of the game, I found myself in the press box at Ratliff Stadium in Odessa, Texas. Our team, a class AAA school, played Fort Stockton, a class AAAA School. In other words, Fort Stockton was a larger school and should have had the advantage over us in an athletic contest. The towns were a couple of hundred miles apart, so we met to play in Odessa.

On the second play of Josh's first varsity football game, he intercepted a pass and ran it back about ten yards. Remember, now, that I was on the radio, and even though I am not a professional, I did try to maintain some semblance of calmness. I was on my feet, and I think I may have been calling the play as it was happening instead of waiting for the play to finish so I could add the commentary I was supposed to give. It was all I could do to refrain from telling the listeners that my son had just intercepted a pass for the mighty Mustangs! I was so proud. I was emotionally invested.

As luck would have it, the game was well in hand before halftime. I don't remember the score, but Josh was the backup quarterback, and the coaches put him in the game to finish up the first half. On his second play as quarterback, he dropped back to pass, I was holding my breath and screaming on the inside. I could see that he had time to throw and that he had an open man. He saw the receiver streak down the left sideline and turn toward the middle of the field. The ball traveled to the end zone, forty yards away, and was caught! By the wrong receiver...interception.

That was a hard pill to swallow. Only moments before, I'd had a smile on my face as big as Texas. My son had intercepted the ball. Now I was lower than a snake's belly in a wagon rut. My wife's son had been intercepted. Well, that's not exactly how I felt, but my emotion of devotion to my son had swung to the opposite side. I had gone from an excited state to mental agitation in a short period of time. I didn't disown Josh. No, he was still my son, and I proudly proclaimed him as such even though he had shown himself imperfect.

I felt for my son at that moment. In fact, I may have hurt more than he did. We all want our children to be perfect. So what do you think God feels like? What do you think He wants? He wants perfection, too, but He knows it's impossible. He knows every child of His is going to throw an interception. It's what we do after the interception that shows who we are and what we're made of. We have to get back in the pocket and throw the next pass. We have to pick ourselves up and forget the sin we left behind as we begin to live for God again. That's when God reaffirms, "This is my son."

I thought I did a pretty decent job on the radio that night. I really thought I held my emotions in check through the ups and downs of the game. However, the next morning when I was in the coffee shop, I heard some of the men discussing the game. "Hey, Kent," one of the men said. "I heard you on the radio last night."

"Oh, really?" I replied.

"Yep," he said. "I thought you did a good job up until Josh threw that interception. Then you kinda went downhill!"

GIVING OUR ALL IN WORSHIP

Continuing with the idea of our emotions, have you ever been a part of something you thought was doomed from the start? If so, what kind of effort did you put into it? Was it a wholehearted or a half-hearted effort? When you go to worship and you have already made your mind up that it isn't going to be worth much, what kind of effort do you put into it?

One more sports story, and then I'll let you and Josh rest for a while. In basketball there were teams we were expected to beat and teams we were most likely not going to beat. The Brownfield Cubs was one of the teams we were most likely not going to beat. In order for us to win it would take our best effort, but the boys just didn't seem to have it in them one night as the Mustangs played the Cubs. Instead of the players exhibiting positive emotions, they allowed their negative feelings to flow freely. Josh seemed to be the most affected. I could tell that he didn't think we could beat them, and his play showed it. He was going through the motions and looked like he just wanted it all to be over as soon as possible.

How many times do we attend worship and not give it our best because we lack peace in our lives? Because of our heavy heart or bad attitude, we don't bring God our best. You know what? When we don't bring God our best, we don't bring others our best. We distract them from the kind of worship they should offer God—the kind that would edify their lives. Those things are important.

I want to give you a "Grump-ism." This is a Kent quote; you can write it down: "The only body that has no emotion is a dead one." Think about it. Based on the definition we discussed, emotion is mental agitation or an excited state of feeling. We should all have feelings about the events that occur in our lives. If we don't, we're dead.

I believe this was what Jesus was saying to the church at Laodicea in Revelation chapter three. If I can put this in my own words, I believe He was saying to them, "I know your work. You think you're rich, but you're poor. You think you can see, but you're blind." Do you know what Laodicea was known for at that time? It was the medical capital of that region. They specialized in the treatment of eye problems. The Laodiceans prided themselves on being able to help people see. Yet here, Jesus tells them, "You're poor, wretched and blind." And He says, "I wish that you were either hot or cold, but since you're lukewarm, you're doing more damage than good."

I think a lukewarm person is a dead soul with no emotion. Even if you go to church every Sunday morning,

Sunday night and Wednesday night, if you don't have any emotion, you're dead. That's the only way I see it.

Does the following conversation sound familiar? I hope you haven't participated in a discussion like this, but I'm sure you've heard similar talk:

"Oh, man, I'm glad that service is over."

"Yeah, it didn't do much for me."

"I couldn't believe Bubba led singing. I don't like it when he leads singing."

"I know. And did you see what Suzy Q was wearing? Who does she think she is? And what about all those people who show up with all of their jewels, trying to show off how rich they are? I can't believe that. It's sickening to me."

"Did you see that guy who looked like he slept under a bridge last night? What's up with that? Man, bring your best, you know? He came to church wearing shorts! I don't understand that. And have you ever noticed how that one guy changes his voice when he leads prayer? You know he's putting on a show. It turns me off when he tries to use that 'reverent' voice."

"Yeah, and I'll be glad when the minister finishes this sermon series. I'm ready for something else. Oh well, at least we can cross church off our list for the week. We did what we were supposed to do."

Oftentimes when we attend worship, we do it because it's "the law." We show up and check our cards three times for three church services. Sunday morning—check; Sunday night—check; Wednesday night—check. We are like the Israelites in the Bible. The Old Testament records countless times when God's chosen people turned away from Him. The Bible talks about how they did things only because they were required to do so by the law. Then they added traditions on top of the law, and their traditions became law. They just punched their time cards. They kept the law, but they didn't give God what He really wanted: praise, worship, and honor.

It reminds me of that old hymn, "Oh, the bitter pain and sorrow that a time could ever be, when I proudly said to Jesus, 'All of self, and none of Thee.'" Have you been at that point in your life? But when you started giving God some of yourself, what did it do for you? The last verse of that hymn talks about "none of self, and all of Thee." In other words, we're to give God everything we have.

BREAK-THOUGHT

So, how are we going to get excited about things? Let me tell you something I've learned. In the last chapter, I told you about a visit I had with Vance Bryan and how he counseled me. I was pouring my heart out when, all of a sudden, Vance took me to his backyard to look at his flowers. I thought it was strange at the time, but then I realized he was making a point. He was showing me the wisdom in keeping my mind still.

I learned another gem of truth from Vance that relates to our topic about the emotion of devotion. A "Vance-ism," if you will. I want you to remember it, because it has been the number one tool for me the last couple of years. It is just these two words: "break-thought." Think about it. Whatever you're thinking about that's taking you away, break-thought. I've been trying to exercise this concept. When I have negative vibes, I just break-thought. Vance told me, "One of these days, it will become natural. You won't have to tell yourself, *break-thought*. It will just happen. You'll break-thought."

A prime example of this happened to me the other day when I was in Target. As I was walking out, I saw a couple standing at the customer service desk. They each must have been about 20 years old. The guy had yellow hair with black spots and was wearing pants large enough for six people to fit in. He was sporting a spiked collar and wristbands and had earrings hanging to his shoulders. The girl's head was mostly shaved, but she had the most perfect spikes in the middle of her head all the way from the front to the back. The spikes had to be at least 10 inches high. And they were purple. She was wearing an unbelievably short skirt and was displaying tattoos all over. I sarcastically thought, *Good night! I bet their parents are proud of them!*

About that time, it hit me—break-thought. What was I doing? I was passing judgment on two people based solely on their appearance. So I decided that they must be on their way to a costume party. I walked out of Target with a positive attitude about those kids instead of a negative one. Let me tell you, that's a pretty big stretch for an old boy like me. I come from a little town in West Texas, and seeing something like that scares me. I had nightmares that night, but at least they were positive nightmares!

So, I've had to learn to break-thought. When I attend worship on Sunday morning, Sunday night, or Wednesday night and find my mind wandering on occasion, I tell myself to break-thought. Over time, it's become more natural for me to do this and get my mind back on track.

Some people have no trouble with this. I remember Mary Horner, a sister from Denver City, who's since moved to Brownfield. For every class I ever taught and every sermon I ever preached at Denver City, Mary always sat three rows back, right in the middle. During every lesson I presented there, I could see her nodding and saying, "Oh, yes. Oh, yes." She was giving me the strength and support I needed to carry on. Mary didn't have to check herself with the break-thought concept; she was with me one hundred percent.

I taught the old folks' class in Denver City. They were the saints who came to the auditorium Sunday morning and couldn't make it any farther than the back three rows, so we had class right there. I jokingly called them the "Cardiac Care Unit." (If you're wondering, I called them that in person, and they just laughed.) They were the sweetest people. I love teaching older adults. You know why? They are either with you or asleep. You won't receive vacant stares from older folks, and they don't count the bricks on the wall. They're either with you and support you, or they're snoring.

I was teaching that class one Sunday morning with a portable microphone that was notorious for malfunctioning. When the batteries went dead, there was no telling what would happen. It picked up radio stations and static, just went dead, or sometimes transmitted high-pitched feedback that would pierce your ears.

I was talking and made what I thought was an extremely good point. I have to admit, I impressed myself! All of a sudden I heard, "Praise God!" I realized my microphone had died because the "Praise God" came over the speakers of our sound system. I knew the exclamation wasn't from anybody in my classroom. I'm not sure where it came from. There must have been a group of people praising God down the street and our sound system somehow tuned them in. I just about fell out of my chair and I wasn't even sitting down! I knew my point was good, but to get a response from outside the building? Whoo! That was powerful stuff. But you know what? Those people, whoever they were, were praising God. They were emotionally excited.

THE FRUIT OF THE SPIRIT

So, how can we do that in our lives? With the help of God, we can strive to live out the principles we find in Philippians 4:4–8:

> Rejoice in the LORD always. I will say it again: Rejoice! Let your gentleness be evident to all. The LORD is near. Do not be anxious about anything, but in everything, by prayer and petition, with thanksgiving, present your requests to God. And the peace of God, which transcends all understanding, will guard your hearts and your minds in Christ Jesus. Finally, brothers, whatever is true, whatever is noble, whatever is right, whatever is pure, whatever is lovely, whatever is admirable—if anything is excellent or praiseworthy—think about such things.

Whatever is pure—that's how you start bringing what you should to God, by thinking purely. If you're thinking about purity throughout the week, guess what? You become pure. Luke 6:45 has a few things to say about how what we store up in our hearts and minds will eventually come out in our actions:

> The good man brings good things out of the good stored up in his heart, and the evil man brings evil things out of the evil stored up in his heart. For out of the overflow of his heart his mouth speaks.

What's in your heart and mind? If you're sitting in church thinking about making more money next week or about how the kids are going to do in their ball game—by the way, I've done that—or about that boy or girl next to you and how you'd like to go out on a date with him or her, you know what? Your heart and mind are not in the right place. I'm not saying any of these things are wrong in and of themselves, but when you're coming to worship God, focus on God.

If you have pure thoughts and are thinking about God on a daily basis, it's so much easier to say no to the things you need to avoid. Romans 8:5–6 gives us more insight on this mindset:

> Those who live according to the sinful nature have their minds set on what that nature desires; but those who live in accordance with the Spirit have their minds set on what the Spirit desires. The mind

of sinful man is death, but the mind controlled by the Spirit is life and peace.

So, how do we live as the Spirit would have us live, and how do we set our minds on what the Spirit desires? Galatians 5:22–23 tells us what we need to cultivate in our lives in order to fill our lives with the Spirit rather than our own selfish desires:

> But the fruit of the Spirit is love, joy, peace, patience, kindness, goodness, faithfulness, gentleness and self-control. Against such things there is no law.

We should all know and practice the fruit of the Spirit. When we think on those things, we are able to incorporate them into our lives. Once they become a part of us, our lives are so much better.

Richard Beasley, a brother in Christ I esteem highly, has shared with me how he feeds himself spiritually. He tunes in to Christian music on the radio or listens to a biblically centered audio book or an uplifting speaker on CD. These tools help him stay focused on where he needs to be and nourishes his relationship with God.

Some time ago, Paula and I cancelled our subscription to *The Dallas Morning News* because the paper started publicizing gay marriages and other gay relationships. Let me tell you, that was one of the best things we ever did to eliminate distractions that kept us from focusing on God and seeking spiritual food. You know why? I used to spend forty-five minutes every morning reading the sports section. I knew everything, even about the peewee teams in Collin County. You know what I do now? I read God's Word, pray and sing.

Most every morning when I wake up, I have praise songs to God in my head. I have prayers on my mind for my family, my congregation, and others. God is the first thing that is on my mind. And when I'm driving, I find myself humming spiritual songs. These uplifting moments have become a part of my routine, and now they come naturally.

Does this mean I have distractions and temptations whipped? No. Can I go back where I've been? Certainly. It would be easier to return to my old habits than it would be to stay where I am. I'm a sinner, just like an alcoholic is an alcoholic. I'll fight sin every day of my life, but the closer I move to God and the more involved in worship I become, the easier it is for me to keep Him at the forefront of my mind.

If you want to become more emotionally involved in worship and strengthen your connection to God, meditate on the words of Galatians 2:20. This verse offers a concept we need to put into practice—to live every day for Christ and not for ourselves:

> I have been crucified with Christ and I no longer live, but Christ lives in me. The life I live in the body, I live by faith in the Son of God, who loved me and gave himself for me.

So, I invite you to consider what we've talked about: excitement in worship, the emotion of devotion, and what we bring to the table. You know, a worship service is exactly what you bring to it. It's what you make it. It's what your mind allows in. When you imagine, what do you think about? When you dream dreams, what are they? Let me tell you, my dreams have changed for the better.

There's a song from a few years ago that has touched me, and it has obviously touched a lot of other folks as well because you wouldn't have expected to hear it on country, pop, or rock radio. It has received extensive airplay, and it's amazing. It has touched my life so much because the message is so powerful. The song is called "I Can Only Imagine," by Mercy Me. That song sends chills all over my body and brings tears to my eyes as I allow myself to think about the day we will see Jesus and what it will be like. I don't know if I'll dance or be frozen in silence, but I do know that if I want to spend eternity with Him, I need to become more emotionally involved with Jesus today.

That's emotion. Bring it every time, and not just to worship. Bring it to your spouse and children. Bring it to those you love, and bring it to those you don't know. Show them the love of God. Show them so they can imagine Jesus just like the song says.

THREE
HOLY GROUND

What is holy ground, and what does it mean to us? To set up this topic and illustrate my points, I want to start with a story.

In October 2003, I made my first trip to Honduras. John and Pat Hendry organized and led the trip. John has been the deacon in charge of missions at my home congregation for several years. Bob Walters, an elder from the LaGrange Church of Christ in LaGrange, Georgia, accompanied us. I had been to foreign countries before, but never to Honduras. I'd heard stories about Honduras from others who had gone to serve there for many years, and I'd seen photos from mission reports, but I wasn't particularly prepared for what I was about to see and experience.

We left home at 4:30 a.m. on Friday to catch our flight via Miami and arrived in Tegucigalpa, the capital of Honduras, around noon. When we got off the plane and went through customs, I noticed a hoard of people. As we walked out, we were smothered by aggressive locals who all wanted to help us with our bags. Every person who touched our bags expected to be paid, so we told them, "We don't need help."

We finally loaded up in a truck that took us toward Gualaco. The drive from the airport to the outskirts of Tegucigalpa, the largest city in Honduras, was an eye-opening experience. We saw people living in tin houses constructed of posts, boards, and rusty corrugated metal. When I was growing up, my pigs lived in better places than that, so I was shocked.

As we slowly made our way, we drove on dirt roads so terrible you could lose a wheel from the potholes. When we arrived at the church building in Gualaco that night, the congregation was expecting us and opened the gate for us to drive in. We got out of the truck, and I was greeted by more Hondurans than I ever thought possible. They were all hugging me, crying, saying hello and telling me how glad they were to see me. (At least that's what John Hendry told me they were saying.) It was Friday night, and they were worshipping.

We asked, "What's happening?"

"Oh, it's Friday night worship," they said.

"Are you holding a gospel meeting?"

"No, we do this every Friday evening. And tomorrow night, we'll have a small group study."

That night, we stayed in dormitories built on the side of the church building. On Saturday, we were given an opportunity to acclimate to our surroundings, and on Saturday night, we went to Big Santo's house. That was the meeting place for the small group study, which included basically the same hundred people from worship Friday night. Of course, they wanted to host us in their living room. So we squeezed in shoulder-to-shoulder and elbow-to-elbow with these gracious people who loved us just because we were there. The people were enthusiastic and said "amen" all the time. It was unbelievable.

WHAT IS HOLY GROUND?

Over the next twelve days, we made trips to different villages to visit local congregations. During this time, I saw and experienced things I could have only dreamed about. On the first Sunday morning, we went to Pacura to worship with their congregation. A family we met there told us they walked four hours one way just to worship every Sunday. Talk about dedication and desire! The emotion of their devotion was evident. John Hendry preached, and we had communion and sang. I noticed how difficult it was for me to recall the words to the songs I had known all my life, because they were singing them in Spanish. The singing was beautiful, but as I tried to sing with them in English, the words wouldn't come. So I found myself humming along.

That afternoon, we traveled around to different people's homes. First, we visited the home of a Honduran sister in Christ and her mother. The McDermott Road congregation in Plano, Texas had built them a house a year or two before. The house was one room, only about 15 by 30 feet, with a kitchen and outhouse in the back. The daughter, ill with a high fever, was lying on the floor, and her mother had covered her with blankets. Chickens, pigs, and dogs were also running around in the house.

After that, we went to other homes to give shoes and clothes to children. We all crowded up on the porch of one family's house. The husband was a mechanic who worked in another town. He rode the bus Monday morning to work, and he rode it back home on Friday night. He had a corn-grinding machine attached to a motor, and he proudly demonstrated to us how he made corn mash. The people of Pacura paid him for freshly ground corn to make their tortillas. The wife taught at the kindergarten, a building with corrugated metal on the sides, located right next to their porch. Their children were beautiful, but dirty. I had noticed their little girl at church that morning because she was wearing a cast on one of her legs. Standing in the middle of us was her baby brother, naked from the waist down.

John Hendry said a few words as we stood there on the porch, and then we began to sing. I looked around at the children and the school building. A sow, dirty from head to toe, was rubbing up against the side of the building. Dogs were barking, chickens were running around, and a donkey with a broken leg was also standing there. I was trying to remember the words to the song, but I couldn't recall them. I was humming and looking around at this beautiful place. It was green with hills and natural beauty in all directions.

We started to sing the words of the next song: "We are standing on holy ground. And I know that there are angels all around. Let us praise Jesus now. We are standing in His presence on holy ground." Do you know what happened to me when I heard that song and realized what we were singing? I started crying. I tried not to let anybody see, so I turned my back to the crowd and looked at the country-side. I thought, *We're standing on holy ground.* Perhaps for the first time in my life, it made me consider, w*hat is holy ground?*

From the time we arrived in Honduras on Friday at noon

until Sunday afternoon, I had been wondering, *what in the world am I doing here?* Just then, it dawned on me what I was doing there. I had come to help people who were helping me more than I was helping them. I realized at that moment we are all capable of standing on holy ground. I thought about what I had at home and how many times I had avoided the idea that where I lived could be holy ground. I had failed to realize that God had given me the privilege of standing on holy ground on a daily basis.

These people were so poor that if I had been them, I would probably have sat in a heap of ashes like the people in the Old Testament, just begging the Lord to let me die, saying, "Please take me, it's just not worth living like this any more." But you know what? These people went to church on Friday night, met together in small groups on Saturday night, worshipped on Sunday, and got together again on Monday. The ladies even brought their kids to learn songs on Tuesday. Do you know what they did every day? They praised God.

I was reminded of Acts 2, which talks about the early Christians and how they gathered together daily to share what they had with one another and grow in the Lord. Most of the Honduran people we met didn't have the distractions of western culture. However, it's getting there—Gualaco had just received cable TV, and Pacura had it as well. The preacher in Pacura lived with his family in one tiny room in the back of the church building. A quilt divided the bedroom from the kitchen and the living room, and I was surprised to see that a cable for TV had been strung in there.

We discovered something really sad on Sunday night. It was an hour and a half drive from Pacura back to Gualaco, and we were going to work on that end of the valley for two or three days, so we decided to stay in a hotel in San Esteban instead of driving all the way back. It was a nice place, and I shared a room with Bob Walters. As we scanned what was on TV, we were shocked to find that one out of only eight channels available was showing pornography. Western culture had arrived. I realized they have distractions and temptations just like we do. They have to make the same choices that we have to make.

HOLY GROUND
IS WHERE THE LORD IS PRESENT

Let's open the Word of God to Exodus 3:1–6 to see what the Lord has to say about holy ground. I'm sure you'll recognize this passage:

> Now Moses was tending the flock of Jethro his father-in-law, the priest of Midian, and he led the flock to the far side of the desert and came to Horeb, the mountain of God. There the angel of the LORD appeared to him in flames of fire from within a bush. Moses saw that though the bush was on fire it did not burn up. So Moses thought, "I will go over and see this strange sight—why the bush does not burn up." When the LORD saw that he had gone over to look, God called to him from within the bush, "Moses! Moses!" And Moses said, "Here I am." "Do not come any closer," God said. "Take off

your sandals, for the place where you are standing is holy ground." Then he said, "I am the God of your father, the God of Abraham, the God of Isaac and the God of Jacob." At this, Moses hid his face, because he was afraid to look at God.

What was it that made the place Moses was standing "holy ground"? It was the presence of God. God was in the burning bush. God had clearly protected Moses from birth to bring him to this moment. When Moses saw this bush burning and went to find out why it was not being consumed, God told him to take off his sandals because he was standing on holy ground. That's where the Lord was.

There's another great example of holy ground in the Old Testament. Genesis 28:11–17 gives us the account of Jacob's encounter with God:

When he reached a certain place, he stopped for the night because the sun had set. Taking one of the stones there, he put it under his head and lay down to sleep. He had a dream in which he saw a stairway resting on the earth, with its top reaching to heaven, and the angels of God were ascending and descending on it. There above it stood the LORD, and he said: "I am the LORD, the God of your father Abraham and the God of Isaac. I will give you and your descendants the land on which you are lying. Your descendants will be like the dust of the earth, and you will spread out to the west and to the east, to the north and to the south. All peoples on earth will be blessed through you and your offspring. I am with you and will watch over you wherever you go, and I will bring you back to this land. I will not leave you until I have done what I have promised you." When Jacob awoke from his sleep, he thought, "Surely the LORD is in this place, and I was not aware of it." He was afraid and said, "How awesome is this place! This is none other than the house of God; this is the gate of heaven."

Why was Jacob able to say, "Surely the Lord is in this place?" Because he saw God's presence there. He knew God was in that place. He understood that God had spoken to him through the dream and that he had seen the Lord with his own eyes. When he woke up and realized what had happened, he was frightened because he was on holy ground—ground where God was present.

Now, you may be saying, "That all sounds good, but how exactly does the idea of holy ground relate to me?" Well, I believe that any place where God is present can be called holy ground. I also believe that God is with us wherever we are at this very moment. A church building is no more holy than our back porch or our living room. God is present in all those places.

In the Great Commission, Jesus told His disciples to go about preaching and teaching all over the world. In Matthew 28:20, He told them, "...surely I am with you always, to the very end of the age." Yes, He was talking directly to the disciples, but He was also talking to us. God is going to be with us. Jesus talked about sending the Comforter, the Helper, who we know is the Holy

Spirit. The Word of God tells us that Jesus is God and that the Holy Spirit is God. It's difficult for us to get our minds around that concept and, I admit, I still don't fully understand it.

I once heard a story that the beginning of eternity is like an ant walking around the equator until it cuts the earth in half. Well, that doesn't mean a lot to me, because I don't understand how something goes on forever. I don't understand how eternity never began, and never ends, and I don't understand how God, Jesus, and the Holy Spirit are all the same entity. But do you know what? It doesn't matter, because they are—and praise God that they are! Praise God that those three personalities are such that we can connect with them.

THE INDWELLING OF THE HOLY SPIRIT

In 1 John 3:1, the writer says, "How great is the love the Father has lavished on us, that we should be called children of God! And that is what we are!" So, we are not only *called* children of God, we *are* children of God! Now, if we are children of God, are we not welcome in our Father's house and at our Father's table?

You know, there is nothing better to me than having my grown son and daughter come home to visit. They're welcome in my home because they're my children. True, my children have messed up, but no matter what they've done, they're still my children. They're on my "holy" ground in my house because they're special to me. In the same way, we are on holy ground in God's house because we are His children. He has sent the Comforter to us, and He says in Acts 2:38 that when we put Jesus on in baptism, we will receive the gift of the Holy Spirit.

I was raised in a congregation that taught the only way the Holy Spirit can dwell in people is through the Word. It's true that the more we know the Word the more we have the Spirit of God in us. But, brothers and sisters, I believe that when we put on Christ in baptism, we are given the indwelling gift of the Holy Spirit. He lives in us every day. And if the Holy Spirit lives in us, guess what that means? Where we are is holy! Have you thought about that?

Maybe some of you guys will understand this. I once heard a kid say, "You won't believe it, but one of the greatest smells in the world is a football locker room." Man! Have any of you ladies ever gotten close to the door of a football locker room? Well, if it's important to you, and if it's where your emotions are, you can smell the sweat, grass, blood, camaraderie, and team effort there. And if you think about it, God is there too—if you're His child.

A sophomore linebacker on the football team (we called him "Musclehead") attended our church. He once told me, "I just love our team captain, our quarterback. Even if we travel, we get always get to the dressing rooms a couple of hours early, and the coaches tell us, 'Men, you've got to start psyching yourself up for the football game.' So our quarterback puts on his football pants and his T-shirt and sits down in front of his locker to read the Bible." How inspiring is that? A locker room is a place to teach. A locker room is holy ground. A locker room is where you and the Spirit that dwells in you can display

God and Christ through your life. By doing so, you might be the only glimpse of Jesus someone ever sees. So where does that take us? Well, I think we have to realize that if the Spirit indwells us, and if where we are is holy ground, we've got some thinking and soul searching to do.

When I was growing up, I did things I knew I shouldn't do if I was pretty sure I wouldn't get caught. Have you ever done that? I think this was one of the main reasons Jesus sent out His disciples in groups of two—for accountability as well as strength. Ecclesiastes 4:12 talks about two being better than one and three being a cord not easily broken. Some of that strength is not just for fighting off the enemy or refuting incorrect teaching but also for accountability. It's because when I'm with you and you're with me, we're reminded whose we are and what we are—God's children. Don't you find this to be true?

I crashed an airplane one time. Thankfully, I walked away, as did the two other guys with me, but the plane was totaled. A friend who saw us crash came running frantically toward the plane to find us. When he saw me, he said, "Oh, Kent!" and then proceeded to let out a stream of expletives. Then he saw Ray. "Oh, my goodness!" he said, and then proceeded to spew out another lengthy string of profanity. Then he asked, "Were there three of you in there?"

The third man, Jeff, said, "No, there were four," indicating that God was riding with us.

The friend, who had been using the colorful language, pulled me aside and asked, "Is that guy a preacher?" I guess he had picked up Jeff's belief that God was with us on that plane.

Well, he was a preacher, but what difference did it make? If he could cuss up a blue streak with me, why couldn't he do the same in front of a preacher? Maybe that's a reflection on the light I was shining at the time. Maybe I had not been showing him Christ in my life. So I have started asking myself. "Do I act differently when I'm around my minister? Do I put up a false front when playing golf with the elders from my congregation?" I think it's time I realized that one more important than them is living inside of me.

NO LONGER A SLAVE TO SIN

You might be saying, "Well, Kent, I don't understand how the Spirit can be living inside of us and how we're on holy ground. It's tough to comprehend, because we sin." Well, that's right, but it's not counted against us. I John 1:7 tells us that if we walk in the light as He is in the light, His blood cleanses us. Now, verse 9 does say that we need to ask forgiveness for our sins. But if we're living for Jesus as a slave to righteousness, as Romans 6 mentions, it is not our intent to sin. We're going to fall off the wagon occasionally, but guess what? We're not living that way. Have you thought about that? Are you living in sin? You would probably say, "Well, no." Then praise God, because if you are not living in sin, or practicing sin, you have already been cleansed and that occasional sin is not counted against you.

Think about this: Was King David a slave to sin? We know he was a man after God's own heart (see 1 Samuel 13:14). David sinned, but he wasn't a slave to sin. There's a difference.

How about Peter? Was Peter a slave to sin? I don't think so, but we know of three occasions in one night when Peter was clearly in the wrong. Think about the night when Jesus was questioned at the mock trial and tortured. I'm paraphrasing, but members of the crowd said to Peter, "Wait a minute. You were with Him." But Peter swore and said, "I don't know the man!" (see Matthew 26:69–75). Did Peter sin? Yes. But was he a slave to sin? Did he live for sin, or did he live for Jesus?

Not long after this time, Peter stood up in front of thousands of people and delivered one of the greatest sermons ever heard. In Acts 2, Peter boldly addressed the crowd in Jerusalem. He described Jesus and, with a conviction that we are afraid to use today, boldly proclaimed, "You have crucified the Son of God." Peter was living for Jesus. He had failed Jesus when Jesus needed him most, but now Peter took the unpopular and dangerous responsibility of telling those present that they had put Jesus on the cross.

Are we going to sin? Certainly. In Romans 3:23, Paul explains, "For all have sinned and fall short of the glory of God." Then in Romans 6:1, he states, "What shall we say, then? Shall we go on sinning so that grace may increase?" I think the Church has been afraid of the concept of grace because we don't want to get hung up on the 'once saved, always saved' doctrine. If we allow the grace of God to live in us, the question becomes, "Should we continue in sin so that grace can be plentiful?" Paul basically says, "God forbid! Don't test Him that way. You don't do that; you get away from living in sin because you're a slave to God, not to sin!"

Was Paul a slave to sin? I don't think so. After Paul saw the light, I don't think he was a slave to sin (see Acts 9). He was living for God and, by the way, even before he saw the light, he thought he was doing God's will. A lot of people think they're doing God's will but haven't seen the light. They haven't understood.

My meager understanding of Romans 7 tells me that Paul had some problems. He was having some internal turmoil over this issue of grace. He had grown up in a Jewish household, and there was something in him that wanted to fall back on the legalism from his upbringing. But now, he was telling others and himself, "It's okay, we've got grace." Now, perhaps that's a simple view of things, and I may be a little off track. But I think Paul was saying, "Look, I do things I don't want to do." Paul struggled with sin, but he didn't live in sin. So, folks, when we don't live in sin and are not slaves to sin, we are protected from the hold it has over us to make us do the things sin would have us do.

WE ARE LIVING ON HOLY GROUND

Jesus said there would be a Comforter sent to us (see John 14:16), and I hope what I'm getting across is that we are living on holy ground. Some of us are living on holy ground in extreme material comfort. But that's not what it's about.

Some of our brothers and sisters in the Lord are living on holy ground in tin buildings.

When you're at work, consider the fact that you are on holy ground. Then ask yourself whether you are acting as if God is living in you. When you're sitting at the computer and there are all kinds of evil at your fingertips, realize that God is sitting there and that you're on holy ground. When you conduct a business deal and say, "What he doesn't know won't hurt him," realize you're on holy ground. And when you show your children Christ is in your life—or maybe you show them that He is not—ask yourself about holy ground. Look at the responsibility you have to others.

I want to close with Psalm 23. It seems that about the only time we read this chapter is when someone passes away, but let's look at it together:

> The LORD is my shepherd, I shall not be in want. He makes me lie down in green pastures, he leads me beside quiet waters, he restores my soul. He guides me in paths of righteousness for his name's sake. Even though I walk through the valley of the shadow of death, I will fear no evil, for you are with me; your rod and your staff, they comfort me. You prepare a table before me in the presence of my enemies. You anoint my head with oil; my cup overflows. Surely goodness and love will follow me all the days of my life, and I will dwell in the house of the LORD forever.

Talk about eternity! Wouldn't it be nice to know what it

means to dwell in the house of the Lord forever? To get a grasp of what forever is? To understand what forever really means, and to know that it is there for us? I hope you can find a way to experience holy ground and share this amazing concept with those around you each day.

FOUR
YOU want me TO DO WHAT?

When you think about service, what comes to mind? What does service really mean and what exactly is required of us? That's what we're going to talk about now, and I want to begin with a story from John 13. You'll recognize it, but I'll present it as a Grumpy Smith paraphrase. It's one of the greatest demonstrations of service you'll find in the Bible. The setting is the night Jesus is going to be betrayed when He is with the twelve disciples in the upper room for the Passover meal. They have all reclined at the table when Jesus gets up, takes off His outer garments and wraps a towel around His waist. Then He begins to wash the feet of His disciples.

Jesus comes to Peter, who says, "No, you're not going to wash my feet." Jesus says, "If I don't wash your feet, you have no part of Me, and I have no part of you." So Peter, being the impetuous one he is, says, "Well, Lord, if washing my feet is good, why don't you just wash my whole body? Just give me everything."

Jesus basically lets Peter know that he is missing the point. He wants Peter to get ready for service because He was not going to be with him forever. Things were about to happen that Peter still didn't understand, even though Jesus had told him about them. He was saying to Peter, "You don't understand these things, but you will soon.

What you need to know now is that you're here to serve people, just as I came to serve you. Just as I left the glory of My Father, you're here to glorify Me and glorify My Father through service to mankind."

This is an act of service that would make many of us uncomfortable. I, for one, would certainly be uncomfortable with it. But if we take a look at the culture and tradition of that day, we can see the importance of washing feet. When they ate, they were actually in a reclined position, so their feet were not far from the food on the table. They walked on dirt roads, so their feet needed to be cleansed because of the proximity to others in the way they reclined to eat. Normally, when people were invited to someone's house, they were given the opportunity—if it was not done for them—to wash their feet as they entered the house.

I think the disciples knew their feet needed to be washed, but there was nobody there to do it. They might have been saying, "I don't know what we're going to do, but there's nobody here to wash my feet, so I'm going to sit down and eat." They needed a servant to take care of them—someone to do the job—and the only one there to do it was Jesus. Remember, the disciples had argued about who was going to be the greatest in the kingdom. Jesus had told them the first would be last and the last would be first (Matt 19:30). Then He gave them this demonstration of servanthood.

Now, I don't know about you, but there's something about washing feet that just doesn't sit well with me. I can't imagine what it would be like to have to do that. I might be able to stomach the idea of washing someone else's feet if I were wearing rubber gloves and some dark glasses so I couldn't see what I was doing. Jesus did it not only for John, the disciple He loved, but also for the very one who was about to hand Him over to be crucified.

If you're like me, you've read that story many times and probably heard it used in the context of the service Jesus provided His disciples. But Jesus provided an even greater service the next day with His death on the cross. The next day, He took on the sins of mankind. His action made such an impact that the sky was completely dark for three hours in the middle of the day. God had to turn His back on His own Son because His Son had become sin, and God can have no relationship with sin.

Service is exemplified in that act even more than the washing of feet. In comparison, we would almost certainly be more comfortable (as unpleasant as it may seem) to wash someone else's feet. I'd rather serve by washing feet than by giving my life, even though I honestly believe I'd lay down my life for my family or my Christian brothers and sisters.

SERVING THROUGH THE STRENGTH OF GOD

Let's talk about the service God requires and how we can emulate Jesus' example. There's a song with lyrics dedicated to that mindset:

> "LORD, make me a servant, LORD, make me like You. For You are a servant. Make me one too. LORD, make me a servant, do what You must do to make me a servant, make me like You."

We need to make that our prayer. We should ask God daily to give us a servant heart just like His. You may be surprised at some of the angles we'll take as we explore what service includes. In fact, one of the common themes you'll read about throughout this book is love. As I started looking at the subject of service, I discovered that service is really just love in action. It's that simple.

I once saw a marquee for a church that read "work is love made visible." There are opposing views as to whether we are saved by works or by faith. But the way I see it, if you have love and faith, your works are just the outward demonstration of what you are and what you have. Your works are proclamations of a blessed life that others can see. I Peter 4:9–11 gives us insight on how we can live for God by serving others:

> Offer hospitality to one another without grumbling. Each one should use whatever gift he has received to serve others, faithfully administering God's grace in its various forms. If anyone speaks, he should do it as one speaking the very words of God. If anyone serves, he should do it with the strength God provides, so that in all things God may be praised through Jesus Christ. To him be the glory and the power for ever and ever. Amen.

I want you to remember that passage because the sentiment is going to be interwoven throughout the remainder of this chapter. These verses tell us that if we're going to serve, we need to do it through the strength of God and in such a way that it brings glory to God. We need the strength of God in order to serve when we're called.

When I was a kid, I had a little fiction book about farm machinery. In the story, a tractor and other pieces of equipment are sitting in the barnyard at night. The tractor is a bit big-headed and is talking about how he is the most important implement. All the others say, "Yeah, you're important, but how important would you be without us?" Then each piece of equipment talks about its importance to farming and producing a crop. While the tractor is important, without the instruments behind it, he wouldn't get anything done. And while the instruments are important, without the tractor to pull them, they wouldn't be able to accomplish any work.

So we have this concept of working together as parts with different functions in order to accomplish what needs to be done. Now take this idea and transfer it to us. How does it relate? As Christians, we are all members of one body and, as such, we each have our own tasks. We each have different talents, but all of them have to work together in order to get the job done. We have to be a part of one another to accomplish a greater work. Romans 12:6–9 expresses this thought beautifully:

We have different gifts, according to the grace given us. If a man's gift is prophesying, let him use it in proportion to his faith. If it is serving, let him serve; if it is teaching, let him teach; if it is encouraging, let him encourage; if it is contributing to the needs of others, let him give generously; if it is leadership, let him govern diligently; if it is showing mercy, let him do it cheerfully. Love must be sincere. Hate what is evil; cling to what is good.

These few verses focus on developing our God-given talents, whatever our jobs are. As I look at each gift listed, there's actually an element of service in each. Can we consider teaching a class a service? I think so. What about encouraging others? Some people are good at that and have a great bedside manner. I'm afraid I'm not one of them. There are ways to do jobs, and some of us are better at doing certain jobs than others. I'm so thankful there are people who are able to teach little children, because I just don't have the patience. But I do believe God has given me other gifts. We each have a position and should be on the lookout to encourage others to pursue their God-given gifts in order to better serve God and bring Him the glory.

SERVICE AND ATTITUDE

Service. I can't help but think about a time when I was the direct recipient of someone's willingness to serve. In 1999, Paula and I decided to leave West Texas. In retrospect, we were going through a midlife crisis, and I should have just shaved off my mustache. It would have been a whole lot easier. But there we were, not knowing what to do. I had enjoyed the independence of self-employment all my life, so we decided to open a golf shop in the Dallas/Fort Worth Metroplex. At this point, nobody knew our plans, not even our children. We scheduled a visit to the Metroplex and called some longtime friends who lived in Grapevine, Texas, a suburb in the metro area. We told them, "We're going to be there this Sunday, and we'd like you to show us around."

Well, they didn't know what was up, but they met with us Sunday at a restaurant. As soon as we sat down at the table, Mike said, "All right, forget all of this how you been, and we love you, and it's been such a long time stuff. Tell us what you're doing here. Something's up. What's the deal?"

So I began telling them, "Well, we think we're going to move here. We bought a golf store franchise. Now we're just looking at the area to decide where we're going to build it."

We were all excited about this. As we were talking, he reached into his pocket, pulled out his keys and passed one to me. I asked, "What's this?"

"It's a key to our house," he said.

"Well, why?"

He said, "If you're going to do this, you're going to be making several trips here before you move. You don't need to pay for a hotel room. There's the key to our house. You don't even have to call and tell us you're coming. If we're there, fine. If we're not, make yourself at home."

Now that, my friends, is service. They saw a need without us even having to ask. We only saw them every five or six years, but that's the kind of people they were. "Our house is your house." I'll never forget that. For a man to give me his house key was no small act of service.

A few years ago, Landry, one of my cousins from

Lubbock, Texas, called one Thursday night. He asked, "Hey, Kent, we were wondering if you could pick us up at the airport tomorrow night?"

"Well, I guess."

He said, "Well, okay. Yeah, we're going to spend the weekend there, just kind of getting away. We don't know what all we're going to do yet, but we'd like to visit."

"Okay, yeah, I'll pick you up. Where are you going to stay?"

"Well, you know, we can't find a room in the Metroplex, so we were wondering if we could stay with you?"

At this point I'm thinking, *You can't find a room in the Metroplex? I mean, you've got to give me a better story than that. I can throw a rock and hit six hotels with a vacancy sign.* But what could I say? So, I said, "Uh, okay."

"Sounds good. We're just going to kind of hang around, you know. We'll just do this and that."

"Are you flying on Southwest Airlines to Love Field?"

"Nah, we're flying into Dallas/Fort Worth International, and we're going to get there at six o'clock."

Great. This means I've got to pick them up at one of the busiest airports in the country during rush hour on Friday evening, and they're going to stay at my house because they can't find a hotel room.

"Yeah, okay. When are y'all going home?"

"Well, Monday morning."

All weekend, too? "Well, okay, yeah, sure. I'll be there."

Service. I was handcuffed. I didn't want to do it. Man! Give me a break! We had heard them say months before, "One of these days, we're going to come to the Metroplex," but we didn't know they were going to barge in on us like that!

With the kind of service I offered that weekend, I honestly don't think Landry and his family will ever be back. The whole weekend, I treated him with the same bad attitude I had had when he called. He didn't have a car, so he had to use mine. Landry could ask me for all these favors because he would have done the same for me without giving it a second thought. When I look back, his mom and dad (my aunt and uncle) were there for me through all my milestones growing up.

Between my junior and senior years in high school, I made a trip to Brazil through an exchange program. Guess who was at the airport to send me off and also greet me when I came home? My Aunt Earlene and Uncle Raymond. During the 18 months Paula and I lived in Grand Junction, Colorado, right after we married, my mom and dad didn't even come to visit us. But guess who came? My Aunt Earlene and Uncle Raymond. And here's their son, Landry, wanting to share the weekend with me, and I felt like I was going to prison because he asked.

Recently, my sister, Deon, called to tell me that Uncle Raymond had died. The news was shocking. He and I had spent years together working for my dad. We had built dune buggies together, and gone rabbit hunting together. I thought, *Man, I've got to call Aunt Earlene. It's going to be hard, but I've got to call her.* So I got her on the phone and said, "I heard the news. Earlene, how are you doing?"

She said, "I'm doing okay." Then after a pause, she continued, "Kent, you've got to do this for me."

"I have to do what for you?"

"Well, you've got to do the funeral service."

This was an occasion of service I was happy to fulfill. I was actually surprised my aunt asked me to perform the funeral, because they were good friends with the minister at their home congregation. So I pulled out the foot-washing towel, wrapped it around my waist and cried for 30 minutes as I spoke at my Uncle Raymond's service, paying tribute to him.

What was the difference between the two requests for service? One act I wanted to do and felt privileged to do; the other I didn't want to do at all. Service was rendered both times, but my attitude was different. When my cousin Landry and his family came to visit, they were served and enjoyed their time. They didn't spend a whole lot of time with us during their stay, but I wouldn't have spent much time with me either. I'm ashamed to say, I selfishly felt imposed upon, and I wasn't even trying to hide my feelings. But when the call came to speak at my Uncle Raymond's funeral service, there was nothing that could have kept me from being there. I took the towel and washed the feet of those in need.

THE TRUE MEANING OF SERVICE

So, what is the true meaning of service? We get the idea that service requires a lot of effort. Service is a call to duty and, a lot of the time, we're not comfortable with that. But service is something that God commands us to do. Actually, it's not just another "have to" if you look at it with love. So, I want us to examine service from two angles and recognize the blessings of laying our lives down. You might find that you're serving in ways you don't even realize.

One of the areas of service that is perhaps the most visible and obvious is mission work to foreign countries or domestic sites. In the last chapter, I told you a story about my first mission trip to Honduras, and I want to mention again how important it is for me to serve those people in that beautiful country. Wilson Howell, a brother in Christ, is a dentist who volunteers his time and expertise to help the people of Honduras. I have been amazed by his work and the work of the other dentists who volunteer there. It's been enlightening to me, because Josh is also a dentist. When Wilson examines a mouth in Honduras, you can be pretty sure those teeth haven't been brushed.

Mike Phillips, an optometrist and member of our congregation, and his wife, Cirrie, assist the Hondurans with eye exams and glasses. Pat Hendry and my wife, Paula, along with local preachers' wives, provide shoes for adults and children. This last act of service comes pretty close to what Jesus did when He washed His disciples' feet. We're talking about washing bare feet that have walked through yards, pastures, and dirt floors of homes where all kinds of animals live. These women serve by taking those feet in their hands to wash them, measure them and fit them with shoes. It's a beautiful thing.

That's the kind of service we often think requires us to be inconvenienced, because we are placed in less than ideal conditions and without our creature comforts. We picture this type of service as a true sacrifice. Well, let me tell you, I might have thought like that on the first trip, but I don't think that way now because I love it too much. Do you know why? I believe that when we give and offer service, we will get more in return. Look at Jesus' words in Luke 6:38:

> Give, and it will be given to you. A good measure, pressed down, shaken together and running over, will be poured into your lap. For with the measure you use, it will be measured to you.

Now, back in Jesus' day, they used to wear garments with a pouch, kind of like a kangaroo. When they went to the field to gather the wheat, they would fill this pouch. The scripture says that what we receive in return is going to be poured into that pouch and poured into our lap, and we're going to have a lot.

I've always thought that meant that when we give monetarily, we're going to get more back. I do believe that happens, because I've experienced it. Every time, I've received even more in return than I gave. But now I realize this scripture means more than just monetary blessings. I went to Honduras originally because I thought those people needed me. As I told you in the last chapter, it took me three days to figure out that I needed them more than they needed me. They were blessing my life more than I was blessing theirs.

We perform many noticeable acts of service through our church work such as visiting the sick, donating to the food shelter, painting, planting trees, and mowing grass. Preaching and teaching also fall into this category of service. We may not think we're going to enjoy serving, especially if we feel we are going to be inconvenienced, but once we get into that situation, it always blesses us more.

Let's hit closer to home, because there are probably some other areas of service you haven't even thought about. What about your family and children? What kind of service do you give them? Are you a slave to them? I think so. The terminology of "slavery" is not palatable to us. The idea of "service" is a little easier to swallow. But if you think about it, that's what God wants. He wants you to be a slave to Him. He wants you to be a servant to Him.

We've referenced Romans 6 before about being a slave to righteousness rather than to sin. So, isn't being a slave really just the same thing as serving? For instance, when you change a baby's diaper or feed him, you are offering a service because he can't do those things for himself. You might be saying, "That's not service; that's an act of love." Yes. We've just come full circle. As I mentioned earlier, service is really just showing love for others. Service is our love made visible.

Is taking care of your elderly parents considered service? Yes. Why do you do it? You would probably say, "Well, because I love them and they've done so much for me." Why did they do so much for you? Because they were loving you. We've just discovered an endless cycle of serving.

What about comforting people when they've lost a loved one, when someone dear to them is sick, or when they just need someone to listen? Sometimes you don't need to say a word. You just sit there, listen, and hold their hand. Are you providing service? Yes. Service is showing love.

SERVICE AND LOVE

Sometimes service comes naturally, and sometimes we're called to help in ways we didn't previously think of as service. Let's look at 1 Corinthians 13:1–3:

> If I speak in the tongues of men and of angels, but have not love, I am only a resounding gong or a clanging cymbal. If I have the gift of prophecy and can fathom all mysteries and all knowledge, and if I have a faith that can move mountains, but have not love, I am nothing. If I give all I possess to the poor and surrender my body to the flames, but have not love, I gain nothing.

We don't gain anything by serving without love. If we serve and truly benefit others but are kicking and screaming the whole time, there's no love in us. But if we see a need and fill it with open hearts, guess who also will be blessed?

Think about the story of Jonah. Even after he spent three days in the belly of the fish and was returned to dry land, he still grumbled when God sent him to preach against the wickedness of Nineveh. Jonah preached to the people, but he hoped they wouldn't repent because they were an enemy of Israel. But guess what? They turned from their evil ways, and God had compassion on them. So, even when we don't feel like serving, we should do it anyway.

This idea relates to the emotion of devotion we talked about in chapter 2. You know, sometimes I'm just tired when it's time to attend Sunday morning, Sunday night, or Wednesday night service. Wednesdays are especially tough. You probably know what I mean. Maybe you drive straight from work to worship when it would be easier to go home instead. You really don't feel like going, but once you get there, you realize you've encouraged others by your attendance. When you think about it, you probably get something out of it yourself. So, even when we don't want to serve others, it turns out to benefit us and others.

Let's talk about service and slaves who were sold to become servants to a master. Do you think slaves had a choice whether or not to work for their master? I think they did. Look at Joseph. Joseph was sold into slavery and probably didn't go willingly at first (see Genesis 37:25–28) But what happened to him? He served because he had the heart of God, and as a result he ended up running Egypt for the good of God (see Genesis 41:41). His choice to serve in the role he was given blessed his life.

A slave's life is blessed with food and shelter, but what happens if he doesn't serve his master? He might be beaten or even killed. Well, I don't think there's a whole lot of difference in us being slaves to God. Do we have a choice to be slaves to God? Yes. It's our choice to be slaves to God or slaves to sin. What are the benefits and consequences of that choice? If we are slaves to God, we receive eternal life, we are placed in His family with fellow believers and the Holy Spirit indwells us, just to name a few of the many blessings. Now, will we become the materially richest people on earth? Probably not. But what do we have? We've got salvation. On the other hand, if we choose not to serve God, there are consequences to pay, just as there would be for a slave rebelling against his master.

I want to conclude with one more memory from Honduras. On one trip, Mike and Cirrie Phillips brought sunglasses to give away in the optometrist clinic. Patients could choose from styles inspired by *The Blues Brothers* and *Men in Black* movies. It was so funny when we were leaving the town of Lenoris. A little boy, completely naked except for his *Men in Black* sunglasses, was waving goodbye to us. Did those sunglasses do that little child much good? Not a lot. But he loved them, and we couldn't help but feel warmth in our hearts when we saw him.

Service. Answer the call.

FIVE
WHERE NO ONE STANDS ALONE

It was almost time. Anticipation had been building for the better part of a year. Now, the day and the hour were almost here. Excitement was escalating because what was about to happen wasn't the everyday routine in this little girl's life. It didn't even happen once a year. Sure, her family threw her a birthday party every year, but it was just for family. Maybe Grandmother and Granddad and a few aunts and uncles would show up for cake and ice cream, but there were never gifts.

This was a special birthday because it was her sixth. In her family, on your sixth birthday, you got to have a party, not only with family, but also with friends. She could invite her church friends and classmates from kindergarten. It was going to be a wonderful time. So, the girl was excited because for the first time in her life, she was going to have a birthday party with her friends and there was going to be cake, ice cream, balloons, decorations, and gifts.

She had been looking forward to this birthday since the day she turned five. She had woken up that morning to find her cake decorated, and she enthusiastically watched her mom make the ice cream. It wasn't store-bought, no, that wouldn't be special enough. It was homemade ice cream, her favorite kind. She watched the clock as the time approached for the party to begin. Balloons were everywhere, and crepe paper was strung across the lights and around the room.

Only minutes away. Soon she said, "Mom, it's time. Where are they?" Finally, it was well past time. "Mom," she said, "where are they? Where are my friends, the people I invited to the party? Why aren't they here?"

How does Mom respond? How does she tell her six-year-old that her friends have chosen, for whatever reason, not to attend her special birthday party? How does she tell her the heart-breaking news? For the little girl, a day she looked forward to for so long has turned into one she will never forget. She's alone. And she wonders why.

Years pass, and the little girl is now grown up. Only one week after her parents attend her husband's college graduation, she answers the phone to hear the words, "Your daddy is no longer with us. He's passed away." Forty-four years old, and he's gone. And she asks, "Why, God? Why is my daddy gone? Why did he have to die?" She has a husband, but she still feels the pain and loneliness of losing her dad. How do you handle that?

My daddy has always said that the worst thing that could ever happen to him would be to witness the death of one of his children. I'd have to say the same holds true for me. The next worst thing would be the day I have to say good-bye to him. But that's life.

The little girl asks, "Why? Why aren't my friends here?" Now, years later, the grown woman asks, "Why? Why am I alone?" The questions are there. She even asks God, "Why did You let this happen? Why did You allow my heart to be torn out like this? Why have You turned Your face from me?" She may understand more as a young woman than she did as a child, but she still feels alone.

LORD, DON'T HIDE YOUR FACE FROM ME

There's a song we sing in worship that inspired the title of this chapter. You may recognize the lyrics: "Once I stood in the night with my head bowed low, in the darkness as black as could be. And my heart felt alone and I cried, 'Oh, Lord! Don't hide Your face from me.'"

What's it like to be alone? Jesus knows. Jesus went to the Garden of Gethsemane with three of His closest friends and told them, "Stay here and pray. Pray for you and Me, because the time is near." Then He went away to pray. When He came back an hour later, they were asleep. He said, "Can't you watch for an hour?" (see Matthew 26:36–45). I think Jesus felt alone. As He went back and prayed again, we're told that He sweat drops of blood (see Luke 22:44). He was alone. He was talking to His Father, but He was alone. He knew what was about to happen.

The next day, after being tortured, slapped, spat upon, and ridiculed He was truly alone. At that point, as we stated in the last chapter, the sky turned dark and God turned His face as Jesus took on the sins of the world (see Mark 15:33). Jesus was alone. And we saw what happened when Jesus was alone. It was a dark, dark place. Just like in the song I mentioned above, I'm sure Jesus said, "Lord, don't hide Your face from Me."

Psalm 30 is a song of David that expresses his feelings

of being alone and what it meant when God turned His favor back to him:

> LORD, for you lifted me out of the depths and did not let my enemies gloat over me. O LORD my God, I called to you for help and you healed me. O LORD, you brought me up from the grave; you spared me from going down into the pit. Sing to the LORD, you saints of his; praise his holy name. For his anger lasts only a moment, but his favor lasts a lifetime; weeping may remain for a night, but rejoicing comes in the morning. When I felt secure, I said, "I will never be shaken." O LORD, when you favored me, you made my mountain stand firm; but when you hid your face, I was dismayed. To you, O LORD, I called; to the LORD I cried for mercy: "What gain is there in my destruction, in my going down into the pit? Will the dust praise you? Will it proclaim your faithfulness? Hear, O LORD, and be merciful to me; O LORD, be my help." You turned my wailing into dancing; you removed my sackcloth and clothed me with joy, that my heart may sing to you and not be silent. O LORD my God, I will give you thanks forever.

David says, "You favored me and made my mountain stand firm; but when You hid Your face, I was dismayed." Can you think of a time when David might have felt as if God hid His face from him? We're told David was a man after God's own heart, but we know he was also a man of weakness.

Do you remember the story of David and Bathsheba? Do you also remember how David yielded to temptation at the sight of this beautiful woman taking a bath? Being king, David had the power to have Bathsheba, the wife of another man, brought into his bed. He never intended for the encounter to be anything other than a one-night stand, but Bathsheba became pregnant. After this, David failed in every attempt to cover his sin. He ordered Uriah, Bathsheba's husband, to return home from the battle in hopes that Uriah would lay with his wife. After two attempts however, Uriah never laid with Bathsheba. David then felt his only option was to send Uriah back to the front lines of the battle, carrying his own execution papers with him. David ordered that Uriah be placed in the heart of the battle and then abandoned. He put a contract on Uriah's life and had the enemy carry out the kill. Finally, King David was free to marry the young widow and, by all appearances, completely cover his sin. If humans alone had been involved, David would have gotten away with his sin; however, God was involved, and He was displeased. (II Samuel 11:1–27)

So God sent Nathan to have a talk with David. How do you think David felt when Nathan told him the story of the rich man who stole a poor man's only lamb in order to feed a guest? David essentially said, "Well, he needs to be dealt with; he deserves to die!"

Nathan's reply? "You are the man!" (II Samuel 12:7).

Then it hit him. He felt alone and rejected. He suddenly knew he had caused God to turn His face from him because he had sinned by taking another man's wife.

EVERYDAY LONELINESS

I once told a group of business associates that I was teaching a Wednesday night class at my church. They asked, "What are you teaching?"

"Everyday Christianity," I replied. "Observations and life-learned lessons from an ordinary man."

"That sounds neat," they said. "What's it about?"

I explained, "Well, I share my walk with God. My goal is to help people relate to scripture. You know, what God's Word means to our lives today. Next week, I'm going to talk about being alone. You know, it's hard on folks."

"Yes, that's so true," one lady said. "It's amazing how you can be completely alone in a room full of people."

There are times in our everyday lives when situations make us feel alone. These are the times when we feel the need for someone to care about us or understand us. These are the times when we say, "God, I don't really know why this is happening, but I'm having a really hard time handling this."

Going to an Old Testament example, Job must have felt alone when he faced all those tragedies. Job had a large family and many material possessions, but he lost everything in one day (see Job 1). How do you survive that? How do you not just go out and put an end to your life? Job felt alone. He had friends who came to talk to him and try to comfort him, but he still felt alone because they didn't fully understand what he was going through.

Isn't that the way it is with us sometimes? We don't understand why bad things happen to us. Sometimes they are just part of life, while other times they may be Satan's attempts to pull us away from God. The Book of Job tells us that Job didn't do anything to deserve the calamities that fell on him; they were attacks by Satan to tempt him to curse God. But I think sometimes difficulties do happen to us because of sin in our lives, which is another way we experience being alone through separation from God.

Hebrews 12:6 says, "…the Lord disciplines those he loves." We don't like to think about discipline or acknowledge that sometimes God has to bring us back to Him. God has to make us think about where we are and what we are. I think that's why He says it's so difficult for a rich man to enter the kingdom of heaven. It's tempting for a rich man to say, "I'm a rock; I don't need anything. I don't need people, and I don't need God because I've got everything I need." Let me ask you a question. Have you ever known or heard of a happy recluse? (That's not the brown spider, by the way.) I'm talking about people who alienate themselves from others.

THE NEED FOR TOUCH

We can be alone in a room full of people. I can remember a song where the writer seems to be proud of being a rock or even an isolated island. He says he does not want to be touched, and he doesn't want to touch anyone. To me, the writer portrays someone calling for help, after all, who really disdains love? He's been hurt before, so he wraps himself in a cocoon and stays there. And where does that lead? It leads to total loneliness and self-reliant despair.

Touch is vitally important to us as humans. It is especially crucial to newborn babies. In fact, the benefits of nursing a baby go beyond nutrition to include the relationship nurtured through touch. To be touched and cuddled is to receive life.

When my granddaughter, Mary Alice, nursed as an infant, she would rub her mother's side. Even now at three years old, if she can find a way, while you're holding her, to reach inside your sleeve and touch the skin on your side, she'll do it. The touch, gives her comfort and security. Do you know what? We all need that, and we need to provide it for other people because they need it too. Touch.

We need God to touch us when He turns His face from us. When He's hiding His face because of our sin, we cry out, "God, touch me. Let me know; let me understand." Yet, God is not concrete; He is intangible. He is there by faith, so how can we be touched by God? Well, for me, I'm touched by His Word. It takes faith for me to believe in that, but as I'm touched by His Word, there are other instruments that help that Word come to life: people.

When we feel alone in our sin and failure and lock ourselves in our room, not wanting to touch or be touched, guess what we need the most? To be touched, held, and loved by others. One ole guy back home in west Texas used to play pro football, but injuries kept him from playing after a couple of years. Even though he's now more than sixty years old, he's still as solid as a rock. He works out every day. Big guy, linebacker type—you know, six foot three and two hundred-fifty pounds.

When I walk up to him to say hello, it's like going to a

chiropractor for free. He is a hugger. He grabs me and hugs me, and he's so big my feet leave the ground. Paula loves to be hugged by him, because his embraces are sincere. Love just pours out of those massive arms and barrel chest because you know how much he cares. Every time we go back home to visit, maybe twice a year, we get that hug. I used to see him three times a week, so I miss that. You know he's genuine. That's what we all need. We need to be touched and loved. We need to touch and love others.

I once read a story in the paper about a ten year-old boy with muscular dystrophy who received a service dog and a best friend in the process. The golden retriever went everywhere with the boy; he even slept with him. Guess what? The dog touched his life. You know, there's just something special about the relationship between a child and his or her dog. You know why? A dog doesn't know that a child has muscular dystrophy. But a dog is aware that a child needs touching, which makes the dog much smarter than many humans.

We often see people we don't want to touch. I've told you about my trips to Honduras and how Paula washed the people's feet and the dentists examined the patients' mouths. You might say, "Man, how can they do that?" Because of love. It's because of service. It's because they know these people need help. We need to be willing to touch the untouchable and meet their needs. Jesus did.

A TWO-WAY STREET

So, how do we find out what people need? We get to know them and learn what is on their hearts. We find out how people need touching in their lives. We find out what we have to do to help them. We recognize when they're in the dumps and when they're on the mountaintop. We've all been to both places. And when we're in the valley, what do we need? Well, sometimes we just want to be left alone, but that would be the worst thing for us because we need someone to touch us, even when we don't think we need help.

You might remember the song *Angels Among Us* performed by Alabama. The sentiment of the song is that angels are sent to us while we are at our lowest times, and that they provide us comfort and light from above.

Have you ever thought about this? I don't know a lot about angels, but I do believe they're among us, and I believe they touch us, because I believe they're among us in one another, even in people we don't know. Sometimes we touch others and are touched by others without realizing it.

There aren't many passages, especially in the New Testament, that give us a glimpse of how angels are among us. But Hebrews 13:1–2 does: "Keep on loving each other as brothers. Do not forget to entertain strangers, for by so doing some people have entertained angels without knowing it."

Wilson Howell, and I became closer than just acquaintances several years ago when I preached a sermon on love one Sunday morning. After the service, Wilson approached me and said, "You touched me." Before that day, we were acquaintances. Now, we're good friends who share with one another and enjoy one another's company.

Touching is a two-way street. I was able to touch Wilson that day because God gave me the ability to speak His Word. Wilson touched me because he let me know that my message had touched him and made him stronger. It's just like when Mary Alice reaches inside your sleeve to touch your skin. She doesn't understand now, but she's not just receiving; she's also giving. Think about the touch we need—the touch that brings us closer together.

nothing false

Do you remember singing "This Little Light of Mine" when you were a child? It's been a long time for most of us, hasn't it? Remember the motions that accompany the song? You know, you've got the candle out there, and then you've got the bushel on it. I don't know about you, but I've never been real comfortable singing children's songs. What makes us feel different about singing those kinds of songs than two and three-year-old children do? Maturity is partially responsible. Remember the words of Jesus in Matthew 18:2–4:

> He called a little child and had him stand among them. And he said: "I tell you the truth, unless you change and become like little children, you will never enter the kingdom of heaven. Therefore, whoever humbles himself like this child is the greatest in the kingdom of heaven."

What does that mean? Our brotherhood believes one must be born again in baptism for the remission of sins (see Acts 2:38). But have we been short sighted in our view of this passage? Are we missing some other principles? When you are born again, you are a baby again. Even if you're eighty years old you are now a baby in Christ.

Have you ever seen the light and glimmer of innocence

and honesty in a little baby's face? The characteristic is inherent. There's just a glow there. I honestly believe you notice it more as a grandparent than you do with your own kids—or maybe you just appreciate it more. I think I'm more mature now as I look at my grandson, Major, and the smiles on his face than I was when I looked at my son, Josh, and the smiles on his. It's a difference in perspective.

Think about a baby who is too young to be afraid of anything. There's just something wholesome about that quality. Even at two or three months old, babies smile when they recognize you. It's pure, and you see their reaction. There's nothing jaded. Rather than hiding their emotions, they display them openly. Babies have integrity; there's nothing false in a baby. Babies let you know when they're hungry or when they need changing. They are honest, open, loving and caring. If they're not happy, they're not going to act like they are. They're going to let you know.

My point is this: as a new child of God you have become dependent on God. You have become pure in Christ. Just like a baby you have nothing to hide because you are sinless. As long as you remain that way you have no reason to try to cover up your life. Adam and Eve were naked and had nothing to hide until they opened the lie of sin into the world (see Genesis 3). Why, oh why, couldn't they have just stayed naked?

NOTHING FALSE

Speaking of nothing false, Jesus gives us an example of what that trait looks like in an adult. Let's examine John 1:43–51:

The next day Jesus decided to leave for Galilee. Finding Philip, he said to him, "Follow me." Philip, like Andrew and Peter, was from the town of Bethsaida. Philip found Nathanael and told him, "We have found the one Moses wrote about in the Law, and about whom the prophets also wrote— Jesus of Nazareth, the son of Joseph." "Nazareth! Can anything good come from there?" Nathanael asked. "Come and see," said Philip. When Jesus saw Nathanael approaching, he said of him, "Here is a true Israelite, in whom there is nothing false." "How do you know me?" Nathanael asked. Jesus answered, "I saw you while you were still under the fig tree before Philip called you." Then Nathanael declared, "Rabbi, you are the son of God; you are the King of Israel." Jesus said, "You believe because I told you I saw you under the fig tree. You shall see greater things than that." He then added, "I tell you the truth, you shall see heaven open, and the angels of God ascending and descending on the Son of Man."

This passage struck me. Jesus says Nathanael is a true Israelite, in whom there is nothing false. So, I have to ask myself, *How do I stack up against that?* Nothing false. If I want to live out this example, I have to stop and think about my relationship to God and others.

Some other ways to express "nothing false" are to act without guile or deceit and with honesty, openness, and integrity. Jesus knew about these qualities in Nathanael, which made him and his character stand out. Jesus knew him before He ever met him. We'll come back to this point after I share a story.

Tim Pyles, the minister at my home congregation, and I went to play golf one time. Two men we didn't know each arrived separately and ended up joining us on the course. We all introduced ourselves and, shortly after, it came out in our conversation that I was a realtor. As we played a few holes, Tim and I couldn't help but notice that one of the men told a few inappropriate jokes and that his speech was on the colorful side. We decided to let it slide because he really was a lot of fun and didn't seem to notice that we didn't laugh.

Once when Tim and I returned to our golf cart after the guy had told a vulgar joke, I told Tim, "I don't know if I'm handling this right, but I can't wait until it comes out that you're a preacher. This is going to be funny."

"Yeah, I know it." Tim said, "I'm just waiting on him to dig his hole a little bit deeper."

So, Tim and I were on the same page. We played a few more holes, and we discovered the guy was in the dental supply business and lived in Montana. I said, "Man, that's great. I go to Honduras on mission trips, and our dentists only have one special set of cow horn forceps to pull teeth. Our supplier went out of business, so our dentists have to share one set."

He said, "I'll tell you what. Find out the details on the instrument, and I'll get you some in two or three days. And since it's for mission work, well, we'll probably donate them."

"Great! Thanks."

Then I asked the other gentleman about his profession and found out he lived locally. By this time, we were on the ninth hole. No one had asked what Tim did for a living.

One of the guys said, "Well, I've got to go after this."

The other one added, "I do too."

We finished the hole and began exchanging farewells. Tim and I had really enjoyed playing with these guys, and the sentiment seemed mutual. So, I took the opportunity to ask the local guy, "Hey, you said you live near here?"

"Oh, yeah," he replied. It turned out he lived only a few blocks from our church building.

I said, "If you ever get in the mood to hear some really good preaching, Tim is the minister at the Church of Christ on McDermott Road."

"Oh, really? That's fantastic. My wife has been looking for a place to worship, so maybe she'll visit."

"Why don't you come with her?"

"Oh, I will after she decides where she wants to go, I will."

Then the foul-mouthed guy asked, "Are you serious? You're a preacher at the Church of Christ?"

"Yeah," Tim replied.

"That's interesting I am so tired of that denominational &%!&$* where I attend church."

I was amazed. We thought we were going to have a laugh on this guy and that he was going to be uncomfortable once the truth came out.

The guy told us, "Look, I don't have a business card with me, but I'm going to leave one in the clubhouse for you to pick up when you finish golfing." We parted ways, and Tim and I got in the cart and headed down the course. I looked at Tim.

"You know, brother," I said, "that didn't work out quite the way I thought it would."

"No," Tim said, "but you know the thing about it? That old boy is no hypocrite."

Tim was right. The man was no hypocrite. He hadn't put on any falsehoods. He hadn't led us to believe he was something he wasn't. Neither had we. Maybe we should have said from the beginning, "Look, we don't want to listen to that kind of stuff." I don't know, but I left there believing we had planted a seed.

Sure enough, when we got back to the clubhouse, the guy's business card was there. A few days later, I took out the card to e-mail him the details about the dental instrument. When I turned the card over, I saw that on the back he had written, "Thank you so much. You guys made my week." He had been away from home on a sales trip, playing golf with three guys he never met before and might never see again, and he said, "You guys made my week."

Well, let me tell you, that made mine. I e-mailed him what we needed, and he quickly replied, "Thank you very much. I'll find this and get it to you. By the way, the next time I'm in the Metroplex, you guys are going to have to play golf with me." I forwarded his message to Tim, adding, "You know, it may not be long before that seed needs watering."

You never know, but my point here is that there was nothing false in this gentleman. He was not hypocritical.

GOD KNOWS OUR HEARTS

Going back to the passage from John 1, Jesus in effect was saying, "Here is a man, a true Israelite, in whom nothing is false. There is no guile in him." Jesus meant that this man was totally honest and completely forthright. Now, remember, this is a guy who just asked, "Can anything good come from Nazareth?" Sounds a little negative, doesn't it? Look at the way he had automatically judged when he heard that Jesus was from Nazareth. Was Nathanael a perfect individual? I don't think so, but Jesus said there was nothing false in him. With Nathanael, what you saw was what you got. There was no pretense.

What was Nathanael doing as he was sitting under the fig tree? Maybe he was praying that he might be led in the right direction. Maybe he was studying, contemplating his place in the world, or hoping for the Messiah to arrive. Jesus answered those prayers. Jesus saw him seeking, and knew Nathanael was a man of character who stood for what he stood for and believed what he believed.

As a kid—or even as an adult—did you ever slip around and do things that nobody knew about? That's hypocrisy, isn't it? A little bit of something that's not quite true, not quite right? You know, we can fool people for a little while. If that's what we want to do, we can cover up, hide part of our lives and hope it never comes out. We sometimes do that because if the truth ever came out, others might be disappointed in us. But we have to understand that we cannot hide from God. He sees the secrets we hide from others.

The hymn "Just As I Am" is a confession. When we sing it, it's as if our hearts are saying, "Lord, I'm wrong. Take me. I understand my weakness. I see that I've been hypocritical. I understand that I have let my brother down and have fallen short." We often place sins in categories, classifying some as really bad and others as only minor offenses.

Let me tell you what sin is. The simplest definition of sin is to fall short of the mark. It's my belief that my mark may be different than yours. What I am called to do might not necessarily be what you are called to do. The gifts God has given me and what He expects from me are different from the gifts He has given you and what He expects from you. Therefore, if I do something I shouldn't have done or don't do something I should have done, it may not apply to you. Maybe it's not what we would consider a horrendous sin in a big, black category, but I've fallen short of the mark in my life because I've hidden my light under the bushel. Maybe I've even let Satan limit my light to a flicker instead of a real flame. God sees and knows all.

Let's consider the seven churches who received letters in Revelation 2 and 3. We've mentioned Laodicea before. It was one of the richest cities in the world at that time. They were known for their medical prowess, but Jesus told them they were poor. He said He wished they were cold or hot, but they were lukewarm. I think by "lukewarm" He meant that they were being hypocrites.

I'd like to share another personal story to illustrate the point of living with nothing false in our hearts. When I was nineteen years old, a missionary from Blackfoot, Idaho, visited our congregation. He said, "We'd really love some of you to come up and see the work you're supporting." When he said this, the light just came on. I walked up and told him, "I'll be there in February."

While I was in Idaho, I met an amazing girl at a youth rally. I was impressed with the Christianity she displayed at the events that particular weekend, and I wanted to get to know her better. I met her a second time at a youth camp retreat in the beautiful mountains of Idaho. I respected the way she presented herself and the way she seemed to be knowledgeable about Scripture. The second day of the retreat, her sister, Beth, called me over and said, "Kent, Vicky is not what you think she is."

"Really?" I responded.

She explained, "Well, she's seeing a married man." Talk about being blown away! I couldn't believe it. "Yeah, it's the truth," Beth said. "She's been confronted about it, but she won't listen. I'm telling you this because I hope maybe she'll listen to you."

Okay, that was pretty tough. Later on, I was sitting around the fire with Vicky, and, since we were alone, I had the opportunity to bring up the subject.

"I hear you might be involved in something you shouldn't be," I said.

"How do you know that?"

"Well, your sister told me."

"She's such a hypocrite."

"Who's the hypocrite?" I asked.

She started crying, ran outside and sat on a slide covered in snow for at least a half hour. I found her, and we talked a little while longer. That was on Saturday. On Sunday night, we worshiped with a congregation in Boise, Idaho. When we sang the invitation song, she went forward and asked for prayers from the church. Her life was changed, and she never saw the married man again. I take no credit for that, but God must have used me as an instrument to touch her when other people had been unable to get through. I didn't know her heart when I first met her, but God knew what was going on all along.

In Romans 12 and 1 Corinthians 12, Paul tells us that in Christ there are many members but that all function together as one body. So, going back to the seven churches in Asia, Jesus spoke to the congregations as a whole and also singled out individuals when He basically said, "There are some among you who do these evil deeds." Each church in Asia had a reputation and identity, but it was made up of individuals. Jesus said, "You as a church are not all doing this, but if you're not careful, you'll be drawn into it." So, He gave those in the churches guidelines, encouragement and strength to remember the effect that one has on many.

Are we living without hypocrisy? After our encounter with the two guys on the golf course, Tim and I were glad we had portrayed ourselves in such a way that by the time we had played nine holes of golf, we could invite the local guy to visit our worship services. And the colorful guy from Montana must have seen something in us that rang true, because he was willing to help us with our dental supplies and wanted to play golf with us the next time he was in town. We had shown nothing in our lives that would cause us to be ashamed to explain whose we were.

A good friend of mine, Chip Bennett, used to say the same thing to his children every time they left the house: "Remember whose you are." He always said this to them no matter where they were going. He didn't say this to remind them that they were his kids. What he was really saying was, "Remember that you belong to Jesus. Show Him to the world out there."

A GOOD EXAMPLE TO THE WORLD

We have a responsibility to be good examples to each other and to those in the world. It's eye-opening when you realize how visible your life is before God. You can't hide things from Him. Psalm 139:23–24 invites God to examine our hearts:

> Search me, O God, and know my heart; test me and know my anxious thoughts. See if there is any offensive way in me, and lead me in the way everlasting.

God already knows our hearts, but if we ask Him to inspect our innermost thoughts and motives, we're inviting Him in. When we do this, it shows willingness on our part. It's not enough that God knows what's there. We have to admit our faults and be willing for Him to view us through the microscope. We have to acknowledge our weaknesses, because we know we're not what we should be. We have to ask Him to help us see what we need to do to change, remove the offenses from our lives, and start following Him.

What's inside is what controls us. Whatever we put in is what comes out. Jesus tells us that out of the abundance of the heart the mouth speaks (see Luke 6:45). What are we nurturing in our hearts? If we ask God to search our hearts and test us, He empowers us to change.

A CLEAN HEART TAKES EFFORT

In Psalm 51:10, David says, "Create in me a pure heart, O God…" This prayer of David parallels what we were just talking about. But if we ask God to create a pure heart in us, how does that happen? Does God zap us instantly with that quality just because we prayed? No, there also has to be some effort on our part.

Growing up, I had a set of weights in the garage for years. I'd go to bed every night praying, "God, make me stronger. Make me bigger." However, the only time I ever moved those weights was when my mom made me clean out the garage. I'd dust them off and move them from one spot to another so I could sweep under them. I was praying for something, but I wasn't striving for it. It wasn't worth it to me to work for it. I just wanted God to give it to me.

If we say, "God, create in me a clean heart," it's not going to just happen. We have to open our eyes and read the Scriptures. We have to allow ourselves to be fed. How many of us eat only three times each week? If we go from Sunday to Saturday and eat only three meals, how hungry are we going to be? What's going to be inside us? Not much. So we need to ask ourselves how often we have fed ourselves this week in Scripture, prayer, and song. If we ask

God to create in us a clean heart, we have to be willing to clean out what's there, and we have to make a conscious effort to put something good in its place. It doesn't matter how powerful the thirty to forty-minute message was on Sunday; that's not enough food to sustain us for a week. If we don't fill ourselves daily with healthy, spiritual nourishment, worldly junk food will easily take over.

I'm reminded of a beautiful song that ties to the passage we referenced from Psalm 51:

> Create in me, a clean heart, O God. Let me be like You in all my ways. Give me Your strength, teach me Your song, Shelter me in the shadow of Your wings. For we are Your righteousness, If we die to ourselves and live through Your death, then we shall be born again to be blessed in Your love.

Whatever you do, do it in the name of the Lord. Do everything by His authority so that when He looks at you, He can say, "This is my child."

Do you remember the imagery from the baptism of Jesus? The Spirit of God rested on Jesus, and God said, "Here's My Son, and I'm pleased with Him" (see Matthew 3:16–17; II Peter 1:17) Have you ever thought about that happening to you? Have you ever thought about being the child God is talking about?

God does not require perfection to obtain His affirmation. Our earthly children aren't perfect, but we love them anyway and are there to feed and care for them. They're not perfect, so we try to instruct them and point them in the right direction. That's what God does when we ask Him to create a clean heart within us. We just need to realize He already knows what's there and what needs to be changed.

seven
I USED TO SING

What happened to that happy man I used to know? You know, the one who used to make everyone laugh. The one people used to ask to be master of ceremonies at the talent show. He was never too loud. He never tried to be the center of attention. If you asked him, he was always happy to help out.

I remember when he was so easygoing. He had a way of making you feel good when you were around him. He loved to play games. If a group of folks wanted to get together, he was up for it. When you asked him what he wanted to do, he would always say, "Whatever everyone else wants to do."

He was always ready to sing. He walked around humming, smiling, and hugging. It was so natural and easy for him to make others laugh. One time, he had everyone in the car laughing for five minutes straight. All he did was read aloud one wrong word from a sign by a ranch in central Texas: "erotic animals." It really said "exotic animals." If anybody else had done that, it might not have been so funny. Whatever happened to that guy?

Life. That's what happened. He let life kill his song. And I was that guy.

Let's look at Psalm 126:1–6:

When the LORD brought back the captives to Zion,

we were like men who dreamed. Our mouths were filled with laughter, our tongues with songs of joy. Then it was said among the nations, "The LORD has done great things for them." The LORD has done great things for us, and we are filled with joy. Restore our fortunes, O LORD, like streams in the Negev. Those who sow in tears will reap with songs of joy. He who goes out weeping, carrying seed to sow, will return with songs of joy, carrying sheaves with him.

The Israelites had been in captivity for years, and now they were being brought back to Zion. Verse 2 says, "Our mouths were filled with laughter, our tongues with songs of joy…"

I wonder sometimes if I have lost the gift of song and that joyful attitude of singing because I have lost my sense of freedom. Maybe I'm not sharing in the freedom that these brothers and sisters, the Israelites, were sharing. Maybe I don't live like I've accepted the grace that's extended to me. I'm reminded of the book, *In the Grip of Grace,* by Max Lucado. I've read it a couple of times, and it really opens my eyes and helps me understand that sometimes I'm not sharing in that grip of grace as much as I should because I don't allow the Lord to grip me. So, as we look at what God has done for us, we need to get that laughter and joy back. We need to get that singing attitude back. It's all about our attitude.

ATTITUDE DETERMINES ALTITUDE

We've all heard that attitude determines altitude. Now I'm going to share some examples that support this motivational thought.

I once received an e-mail from a friend that said, "I had to break-thought today as I was on the phone with a customer who absolutely drives me up the wall." We've all been in that situation. As I mentioned in chapter 2, we apply this technique of "break-thought" when we find our thoughts centered on anything but God and how we can be godly to others. This principle can help us deal with difficult people and events. It's all in our attitude.

Are you familiar with Nancy Hughes, a character on *As the World Turns?* She used to sing the song, "Oh what a beautiful morning, oh what a beautiful day. I've got a wonderful feeling, everything's going my way." Soap opera characters aren't known for everything going their way, but Nancy used to sing that song with an optimistic approach to the day.

Do you ever wake up and say, "Oh, Lord, thank You for this day"? I went years without doing that. During the time I didn't have a song in my heart, I failed to notice the beauty of each morning. As a kid growing up in west Texas, I remember that all I could hear in the early morning hours was the hum of irrigation engines. When we moved to Denver City, which is in oil country, we would wake up to the sound of pump jacks. You might ask, "How is that a beautiful thing?" Well, that's where we lived, and those sounds represented the livelihood of our community.

The early morning is a great time for us to stop and reflect on what God has done for us and the specific blessings He has given us. Sometimes we're too busy to take the opportunity. But do you know what? When we take the time to listen to early morning sounds, watch the sunrise or observe a bee or hummingbird hovering around a flower, we encounter special moments when our hearts will say, "Oh, what a beautiful morning."

I went through a period when I could relate to the guys on *Hee Haw* who sang, "Gloom, despair and agony on me. Deep, dark depression, excessive misery. If it weren't for bad luck, I'd have no luck at all. Gloom, despair and agony on me." I felt that way for years. I was raised working for an uncle, and I picked up some bad habits from him. It wasn't that he was a bad guy; he just had a sorry attitude. I don't know how many times I heard him say, "If it ain't one thing, it's nine hundred ninety-nine others!"

When you hear that negativity all the time, the next thing you know, it's gloom, despair, and agony on you. Every time something bad happens to you, you ask, "Why me?" You feel as if bad things only happen to you and no one else.

It's all in our outlook and how we accept what life brings. When we're not living with a song in our heart, we tend to take it out on others. We get upset in traffic and with our coworkers. We avoid others because of their irritating mannerisms.

When I was in the cotton gin business several years ago, my partners and I used to treat our clients to a Las Vegas trip every year. One evening, while in Vegas, I was sitting with my favorite group of friends at a restaurant when I looked up and saw a guy I didn't like walking toward our group. I had never been fond of him, and though I might have been able to tolerate him with a song in my heart, I would have never been able to get along with him. He never made it to us, because when he saw the look on my face, he turned around and went the other way.

If we're not living with a song on our hearts, that's the way we affect people. People see if we react negatively to them, and if we do, they go the other way. Only months later, that same man would spend three months in drug rehabilitation. I could have been a powerful resource to help him overcome his addiction if I had reached out to him, but I didn't do that because I wasn't living with a song in my heart.

A few years ago, I was asked to sing in a choir for a breakfast Christmas party at Southfork Ranch. The only problem was we had to arrive at 7 a.m. because the event was scheduled to begin at 8 a.m. On the drive there, I put in *The Best of Bread* and started singing along, because I needed to warm up my voice. When I did, the most unbelievable thing happened—I had probably one of the best days I had that year. You know what I attribute it to? I started the morning with singing. Was it praise to God? Was I singing songs that would lift me up in a spiritual manner? Not really, but they did raise my spirits because I was singing with my heart.

I used to leave my house in the Dallas/Fort Worth Metroplex at 4:30 a.m. every Monday to drive to Austin, Texas, for business. On one particular occasion, even that early in the morning with almost no cars on the road, the traffic signals stayed red for what seemed like eight minutes. Just as my light turned green, the only car I had seen in eight minutes ran the red light on the cross street right in front of me.

I wasn't in a real good mood that morning. As I sat at those long red lights, I thought, *Man, why can't I just go?* Then I told myself, *Obey the laws of the land, Grump.* So I waited. As I navigated the Dallas interchanges, there was not much traffic, but every car on the road that morning managed to get in my way. When I finally got out of Dallas, I was not listening to Christian radio, but guess what song played? "I Can Only Imagine" by Mercy Me. I mentioned how special that song is to me in a previous chapter. It was like flipping a switch. My attitude immediately changed for the better because I had those uplifting lyrics playing over and over in my head for the rest of the trip.

ATTITUDE IS A CHOICE

Our attitude can change. Attitude is a choice. I'm a private pilot, and the first thing they tell you in flying school in addition to "attitude determines altitude" is "altitude is your friend." What this means is that altitude gives you time to overcome difficulties you might encounter. If you're in a single engine airplane and the engine quits, guess what's going to happen to that airplane? The altitude will decrease because the attitude of that plane just changed. The more elevation you have, the more time you have to select a safe landing spot. If you're barely off the ground when the engine quits, you're just hoping to survive.

Proper fuel source is crucial to your attitude and altitude. Even if you want to stay straight and level, you need fuel to remain stabilized. If you want to climb, you need to increase power. An airplane receiving sufficient fuel can gain elevation.

My first flying lesson was at eight thousand feet above Blackfoot, Idaho. All of a sudden, my instructor said, "Kent, just pull that wheel back as hard as you can. Pull it and hang on to it for as long as you can hang on to it."

"Sir?" I questioned.

"It will be all right," he said. "Just pull back."

"Okay,"

We had full throttle, and I pulled back on the wheel. We started climbing, but then all of a sudden, the plane started shaking. The plane didn't have the fuel and the power to stay in that attitude, so it broke over. When that happens, you can stall out if you're not capable of overcoming the challenge, so fuel is key.

Flying is like life. When we're on an emotional mountaintop for a while and getting a lot of fuel, we can sometimes climb too high. There has to be regulation. If we're running on high with no regard for reality, a problem might cause us to stall out and go into a tailspin. But if we're of the attitude that problems are inevitable in life, we will be better equipped to decide where we are going to land if our engine quits.

It may sound funny, but in a way I enjoy flying at eight feet as opposed to eight thousand feet because I have more of a sense of speed when I'm close to the ground. At eight feet, you can see the ground rapidly passing below you, but at eight thousand feet, even when you are traveling at a speed of one hundred-sixty miles per hour, it feels as if you're sitting still. But do you know what? We can't float along at eight feet above the ground in our spiritual lives. We need proper food such as prayer, daily Scripture reading, and fellowship with other believers to maintain our attitude and altitude. If we only spend three hours each week with Jesus at worship services, we don't have enough fuel to fly straight and level at higher elevations. We've got a nosedive attitude. At such a low level, we will find it easy to burn out or even crash.

As I mentioned in chapter 3, I know what it's like to crash an airplane. When my friends and I took off, we thought everything was fine. After all, I had just filled the plane with fuel earlier that day. But somehow, the fuel source wasn't enough to keep us in the air. We never figured out exactly what happened, but we never got high enough to get over those high power lines.

Ever since that crash, I've had a number of vivid dreams about flying. Sometimes I'm in an airplane; sometimes it's just me in the air. In my dreams, there was always a power line or building to fly over, but I had to turn around because I didn't have sufficient altitude. When I headed another direction, I found more power lines and buildings to fly over. I always felt restricted because I could never fly over them.

After working diligently to put a song back in my heart, one night I had a dream about flying, but there were no power lines or buildings. I woke up the next morning and asked myself why this was the case. I decided it was because I had started to put different fuel in my tank. I was focusing on the positive instead of the negative. A good attitude can take you in a different direction when you allow it to. It's your choice.

YOU HAVE TO MAKE YOURSELF GET UP AND GO

Have you heard the song, "I Just Wanna Be Mad," by Terri Clark? Have you ever found yourself in that mood? I've been there. You know, somebody says, "Have a nice day!" and you think, *I don't want to have a nice day! I prefer to remain angry. I'm much more comfortable this way.*

Times like these are when we really need to break-thought. After all, how much fun is it to be miserable? It's not fun, but we sometimes want to bring others down with us. Or maybe we just want to be alone. We don't want to be touched, and we sure don't want to be around someone who's having more fun than we are.

There's an old song called "Husbands and Wives" that talks about pride being the chief cause of marital problems. And, truthfully, pride is often the culprit in many broken relationships besides marriages. What is pride? It's an attitude that you are right, the other person is wrong, and that is the way it is. When the other person is ready to tell you that you're right and he or she is wrong, you'll be okay. What can you do to change this? Well, you can adopt a

GRUMPY SMITH

different attitude. You can remember that people don't all look at things the same way, and that's okay.

Garth Brooks sings a song called, *"Somewhere Other Than the Night."* It's about a farmer who is in a foul mood because it has started to rain. The rain made him stop working in field and go home for what he considered a wasted day. But what he saw when he stepped into the house had an amazing effect on him. Standing in the kitchen waiting for him was his beautiful wife wearing nothing but an apron. Now in my mind this apron is a skimpy little thing, maybe the size of a hand towel, so I ask you husbands out there, how quickly can a man's attitude go from lousy to elated? Yep, suddenly, his attitude changes dramatically, and they end up growing closer together, all because of this "wasted day." In fact, she sees her husband cry for the first time. It's all about stimulus and how we react to it.

Can our attitude change? Yes! It just depends on the stimulus, but sometimes we shut it out. How many times has an opportunity to change your attitude knocked on the door? You opened the door, and it's something you've been praying for, but you slammed the door? It's like the account in Acts 12 when Peter miraculously escaped from prison. He went to a house where believers were gathered in prayer for him and knocked on the door. The servant girl recognized his voice and was so excited that she ran to tell the others, "Peter's here!" without ever opening the door for him. Attitudes can change because of a stimulus. Are we going to accept it or shut the door and go another way?

You've got to "want to want to." Several times in Revelation 2 and 3, we read, "He who has an ear, let him hear what the Spirit says to the churches." We sometimes know what good is available to us, but we don't want to change. Sometimes we've got to make ourselves do things.

I mentioned in a prior chapter how I canceled my subscription to the *The Dallas Morning News* and how I found that time was better spent in daily Bible reading. Now it's part of my routine. How did I do it? Well, I made a choice. I decided that spending time in the Word each day was important to me. At first, the activity may not be a priority for you, but if you set the parameters, you'll get there.

When you're in a low point in your spirituality, sometimes you just have to make yourself get up and go. That's exactly what I had to do when I was struggling with joy and peace in my Christian walk. I didn't want to. I had absolutely no desire. I saw absolutely no reason to do so. I didn't see how it was going to benefit me, but I decided to get up and get out anyway. When you choose to do this as well, do you know what happens? You begin to come out of the valley.

I remember hearing a Christian brother explaining once how he learned to pray. He didn't pray much but knew he needed to, so he said to himself, *I'm going to make myself pray.* He went into his closet, shut the door, sat there and said, "Lord, You know I don't want to do this, but I'm going to pray." And then he started praying. The next day, he told his wife, "Well, it's time. I've got to go in the closet." He went in the closet, shut the door and said, "Lord, You know I don't want to do this, but I'm going to pray." This went on for a while, until one day he went into the closet and said, "Father, thanks for being there." Do you know why he was suddenly able to say this? His attitude had changed because he realized the benefits of what he was doing. He understood the source of the fuel and started soaring high because he was feeding his spirit. Sometimes we have to go through the motions so that we can get to that point.

PERSPECTIVE IS EVERYTHING

A few years ago, my son, Josh, sold his house and moved his family into an apartment. It's amazing how much stuff a person can accumulate over time. It took a full day's work to help Josh take the U-Haul truckload to storage. I got to bed after midnight, and I was so tired the next afternoon that I fell asleep on my couch before Wednesday night class. Would it have been easy to stay there? Yes, but I couldn't. Why? Because I had to teach a class. But do you know what? I didn't have the attitude of "have to." I was excited because of the blessing and the opportunity to teach.

Sometimes when we do things we don't want to do, we suddenly find that we begin to like them. Even that difficult person who had been a real thorn in my side actually turned into a friend when I opened the door, let him in and started treating him differently than an enemy. Things changed between us. When I changed, he changed. Those changes can be made.

When Paula, and I opened our golf store, we had to build out the space. It was a sixteen thousand square-foot building, and we were the first people to use it. The building had glass windows all the way around and probably a dozen doors, so as the work was in progress in the heat of the summer, the contractors would leave the doors open for circulation. Well, this led to birds (grackles in particular) getting into the building, and they couldn't find their way out. Confused, they flew into the windows, breaking their necks. The day we started the project, we counted forty-four dead grackles in the building. They were in various stages of decomposition. Some were already dried up, but some were still juicy. Completely disgusted, I took a bucket and shovel and started picking up all those dead birds. Then I carried them outside to throw them away. After cleaning up the mess, I couldn't see any use for grackles. All I could think about was how ugly, stupid, and worthless they were.

Some time later, I arrived at the store early one morning to open up and spotted something out of the corner of my eye. It was unlike anything I'd ever seen before. Something dark brown, maybe black, was moving on the exterior of my store. Then I realized what it was. More crickets than I had ever seen in my life were all over that building. They were everywhere. As I opened the door, what seemed like millions of them marched like an army into my store. I was horrified. How was I ever going to get rid of those awful crickets? A couple of hours later, guess who showed up? My friends the grackles! I decided that day I liked the grackles after all, because they came to my rescue and ate those crickets. It all depends on how you look at things.

Sometimes what you think is bad can turn out to be a blessing. It can be amazing.

Did you see the movie *Monsters, Inc.?* In this animated feature, the monsters generate their city's power by scaring children, but by the end of the movie they find out that laughter is 10 times more powerful than screams. In our lives, depression can grow and feed on itself, but looking on the bright side is 10 times more powerful. It's all in our perspective.

We all have a purpose, but it is easy to get so pressed down by the world that we forget what we were born to do. Or, worse yet, we forget what we were reborn to do. I'm reminded of Louis Armstrong singing "What a Wonderful World." You know, God gave us the opportunity to be His children and enjoy the wonderful world He created. That's what we were born and reborn to do. Sing to yourself, "what a wonderful world."

eight
Facing Failure

What I'm going to share with you in this chapter is vitally important. I want to say up front that I'm not sharing personal stories about challenges I've faced so you'll feel sorry for me. That's not the intent. It's not about me. It's about God, and it's about you. If I am able to touch one person who has been where I've been, it will be worth it. This is one of those life-learned lessons. The applications will be made as we go.

I was always somewhat successful. But people haven't always understood how I accomplished what I did. For one, I was a little guy; I wasn't supposed to do what others did. However, it seemed that most of my life, no matter what I endeavored to do, I was always successful. And I enjoyed that success. I was never the most intelligent student, but I was never the dumbest, either. I was actually satisfied with being middle of the road. I graduated in a class of sixteen, and I can safely say I was number eight. I never was the best, but I never was the worst.

At the age of twenty-four, I took over as manager of a cotton gin, mostly on my dad's credentials. Because the men who hired me knew my dad, they trusted that if I had questions, I could go to him for the answers. I could get the job done. By the time I was thirty, I served as president of the Texas Independent Ginners Association. At the time, I was the youngest president ever named to lead the organization, which was six hundred members strong.

Previously, as the association's vice president, I once found out that our president was not available to make a presentation before a Senate subcommittee. So, I took over with basically no notes and gave the subcommittee facts and figures supporting our cause. This was the first of several opportunities I had to sit in the capitol building in Austin, Texas, and be privileged enough to speak before Senate subcommittees and House committees on legislation related to the cotton gin industry. Afterward, Representative Richard Smith patted me on the back, shook my hand, and personally thanked me for my presentation.

I'm not bragging, I'm just telling you how easy things were for me. In the twenty years I managed the cotton gin, there were only two or three years that we didn't make money and that was due to weather-limited production. The remainder of the time, we enjoyed a large profit. During my career with the cotton gin, I also served on the school board, the board of directors at a local bank, the executive committee of the Texas Cotton Ginners Association, and the county committee of the Agricultural Stabilization and Conservation Service. I took pride in those accomplishments.

When I was younger, I considered entering the Air Force, but those plans changed when a missionary from Blackfoot, Idaho, visited my home congregation and said, "Why don't some of you come up and visit us?" I've told you that story before. I originally went to visit for six weeks and ended up staying six months. Things just fell into place for me. When I left Idaho, I went into the Adventures in Missions program. That's where I met my wife, Paula, the most beautiful woman in the world.

Several years later…Paula and I decided it was time to do something different. The Lord had been good to us, our kids were grown, and we were ready for a change. So, our midlife crisis was to sell our farm. I had been told all my life you can't quit farming, because you can't afford it. You work all your life as a farmer, and when you sell out, you owe it all to Uncle Sam. But do you know what? We still had money left over to move to the Dallas-Fort Worth Metroplex and open a golf store.

A SERIES OF DIFFICULTIES

Things were going my way. I'd been successful my whole life, and running a golf store was what I wanted to do. I'd never had a boss—and I didn't want one now—so I went into business for myself with some partners. I didn't exactly know what I was doing, but I believed God would take care of me because He always had in the past. Through an upstanding family I knew, I met a man, a PGA professional, who had experience managing golf courses and retail stores. He just happened to be looking for a job. I thought he was a godsend. So I hired him to help me run my business.

Over time, it became apparent that things weren't going as they should with the store. I had given complete control of operations to the new hire and had come to realize that my inventory level and debt were out of control. I even visited a store in Alabama so I could learn how to run my business better, because I knew my store was in trouble. A couple of days after returning, I found out that there was no way to save my store. One of my partners, who had more assets and more cash liquidity than the rest of us, walked in and said, "You're in trouble, and you're leaving. I'm taking over."

Even though I owned the majority of the store, I didn't want to cause problems for the other partners. So I walked out. Mistakes had been made, and I was responsible. I had hired a man on good report and reputation who turned out to be the biggest liar and most dishonest man I'd ever met in my life. I was not in control of the situation, but I was responsible.

This event triggered a series of difficulties in my life that I thought would never happen because I had always been successful. God had always taken care of me, and I had always given Him the credit. I thanked Him for every crop I ever produced. But all of a sudden, things weren't going my way. I left the store and tried to find a job, but I lost confidence in myself because I had failed. I didn't understand what had happened to me because I had never experienced failure before. For the first time in my life, I hadn't been successful at what I set out to do. Maybe I wasn't grandly successful, but I was always comfortable and assured of who I was.

Years ago, I received the nickname of "Little Caesar" on the golf course, and it stuck with me. In my life as a farmer, ginner, and all my other professional and volunteer duties, I was in charge—and people knew it. They knew that if I was in charge, it was going to be all right. But now, success was nowhere to be found.

I was struggling to find a job, so I decided to try the real estate business. During the same time, I was appointed to a task far greater than making a living. I was appointed to serve my home congregation as a shepherd. In the midst of all that, I failed to lead. I was part of an eldership that could not take the congregation where it needed to go. I felt as though I had failed once again.

I am compelled to give you the result of what I felt at the time was a failure on my part, as well as a failure with the entire eldership. In hindsight, it is apparent that God used us to advance and strengthen the church over which we had been given oversight. I cannot divulge what occurred behind closed door that lead the entire eldership to resign. However, I now know that what I thought was a failure, was in reality a resounding success. By humbling ourselves with the knowledge that the church was more important than we were, we allowed God to once again be in control. I am now proud of the fact that God used my brothers and me to strengthen His church.

When a person faces failure, he or she goes through several stages. First, the person might experience denial, and then possibly anger. The next stage is the most dangerous of all: depression. And that's where I went. I went into depression because of the failures I had suffered. I had never been depressed before. I didn't know what it was, nor did I understand it. I thought those who were depressed were somehow weak.

DEPRESSION CREEPS IN

So, how do you handle depression? What do you do with it? How do you face it? How do you own up to it? How do you recognize it? How do you understand it? A journey awaited me that would answer each of these questions.

Do you know what it is to be in despair? Do you know what it is to be in depression? I pray to God you never find out, because it's a hole you can't dig yourself out of. Depression is quite possibly the ultimate perpetual motion machine. Depression doesn't need to be fed from outside, because it feeds on itself and therefore never runs out of food. The more it eats, the bigger it gets. Allow me to give an example. You can put two hundred-fifty pounds of cotton in a bale press and drop a lighted cigarette on it, and then add two hundred-fifty pounds more cotton on top of it and press it all together with five thousand pounds per square inch of pressure. If you take that compacted bale of cotton and put it in the bottom of a swimming pool, it will burn. Yes, it will burn up. It may take weeks or even months, and I don't know exactly how it happens, but the fire feeds itself inside that bale of cotton.

Depression feeds inside a person's mind and eats away at that person until he or she can't function. Many good friends tried to help me, each with heartfelt concern and godly wisdom. But it didn't matter what they said, because I continued to feed the depression.

One day, my friend John Hendry said, "Kent, some-times your 'want to' just has to get up and do it." Even though you don't feel like doing something—I touched on this idea in the last chapter—you've just got to get up and go do it. But that's easier said than done.

I tried to do this; nevertheless, I would end up just sitting at home and thinking...*I probably ought to go see so-and-so, but it wouldn't do any good. I probably need to make some calls to market my real estate business, but it wouldn't do any good. They would just tell me no anyway. That would be failure, and I can't handle more failure. Man, the last thing I need right now is rejection. I can't handle that. So I think I'll just sit here,* and I fed my depression.

I worshiped numerous occasions and punched my card because it was my duty. I praised God because it was my duty. I was going through the motions. And I was so lonely. It wasn't because no one paid attention to me or because people didn't care. It wasn't because I felt God didn't love me. I was lonely because I felt unlovable. Do you understand how one can become unlovable in one's own mind? Have you ever been fed the idea that you are worthless? You might even feel like God is hiding His face from you. I did. Of course, He wasn't hiding His face from me; He was trying to show it to me. But I pushed Him away.

Many people have said, "Kent, look at what you have. Look at your family. You have a loving wife, the most beautiful wife in the world." She has proven that over the last few years, because no other woman would have put up with me. Anyone else would have walked out, because I was not worth living with and not worth being loved.

My kids didn't know what to do, but they tried. Both of my children are faithful followers of God. My son, Josh, teaches Bible classes and, more importantly, teaches his kids. Every night, he prays with his children before they go to bed. I never did that on a regular basis. My daughter, Miranda, and her husband are actively involved in the young married class at their congregation. I felt blessed when I thought about my family, but I didn't feel worthy, and it was still difficult for me to see God's face even though He was showing it to me.

I have two sisters, two brothers-in-law, and four nieces and nephews. We even have great grandkids in our family now. Every one of them is a baptized believer of our Lord and Savior. Man, am I rich? Did something go right for me? Yes. But I didn't see it. I didn't want to see it. I had let my family down. I couldn't support them anymore. I didn't want to support them. I didn't even have what it took to apply for a job at Burger King, because I was afraid they would say, "You're not qualified to ask, 'Do you want fries with that?'" So, I sat…in the dark.

HITTING ROCK BOTTOM

One day, I went to work on a Sunday afternoon to answer phones at the real estate office. "Opportunity time," they call it. It was a good thing someone else was there to cover, because I spent two hours in a private office in the dark crying and shaking uncontrollably. I suppose I came just about as close to a nervous breakdown as you can come. I went home and told Paula, "I think I've hit bottom, and I've got to do something. Something has to change."

My understanding of the Word of God is that those who lead are held to a higher standard, so I struggled

EVERYDAY CHRISTIANITY

with leading song services at my congregation because I was inwardly overwhelmed by my shortcomings. After the failure of the golf store, I was saddled with such tremendous debt that I had to file for bankruptcy. That represented the ultimate failure in my eyes. I thank the Lord for dedicated Christian friends who supported me emotionally and financially when I didn't have the money to make my house payment.

Have you heard the story about the shipwreck survivor who was alone on a deserted island? He asked God to rescue him, but no help appeared. He built a hut for protection, but he came home one day to find the hut on fire. Smoke clouds filled the sky, and he was devastated at his loss. The next day, a ship came to rescue him. When he asked the crew how they knew to find him there, they told him they had seen his smoke signal.

It's easy to get discouraged when things are going badly, but we shouldn't lose heart. God is at work in our lives, even in the midst of pain and suffering. Remember, the next time your little hut is burning to the ground, it may just be smoke signals that summon the grace of God.

SEEKING HELP

I saw a counselor, I talked to my wife and kids, and I talked to my Christian family. I realized that I was like the guy who prayed to be rescued from the floodwaters but turned down a helicopter ride because God was going to rescue him. When he died, he asked, "God, why didn't You save me?" God replied, "Didn't you see the helicopter?"

I was shoving God away, and I knew that there was something in my life that I was missing. So I made a decision I thought I would never make—one I thought would actually be a sign of weakness. I went to see a doctor, and he gave me medication to stop the depression from feeding itself. When I began taking the medication, people began to notice a positive change in me almost immediately. When my children asked what had happened to me, Paula told them, "Your dad is once again the man I married."

Strains of life can pull us down long before we realize their effects. I discovered that my kids didn't really know me, even before my experiences with failure. Isn't it a shame that we let the pressures of life take our personalities and turn us into different people than we once were?

One example of how I changed for the better occurred at my granddaughter's birthday party. Her favorite color was blue, which was the theme for the party, so I decided to spray my hair and mustache blue. The only blue hairspray I could find contained glitter, and even after vigorously washing the color out, I still sported glitter for about a week afterward. You know what? Before I got help, I never would have done that. I wonder how many of us turn down help from others or don't realize the smoke signals we're sending?

WHY DO WE EXPERIENCE FAILURE?

So, why do we experience failure? I believe at times I've had the "Job Syndrome." Job didn't curse God and die, but he did question God. Oh, I've questioned God. If you want to know God's response when we question Him, read Job 38:3, where God says to Job, "Brace yourself like a man; I will question you, and you shall answer me." How does a man brace himself against the Most High God? And yet I questioned Him.

I believe God disciplines those He loves and that my failures served as discipline. I believe my failures were like a fire that was used to refine me. Sometimes the heat was almost too hot. I never would have taken my own life, but I did, at the time, think about how much better my family would be without me because of the mental and financial strain I was putting on them. Now I see where I have been and, praise God, that there is light at the end of the tunnel.

I know many have gone through some of the same things I've gone through, and probably even worse. When we realize that God sends His grace in response to the smoke from our fires, we begin to heal. If it takes Christian counsel and medication to get us there, praise God for the help they provide. And if it takes brothers and sisters who love, care, and pray for us, praise God for those brothers and sisters! Amen?

I praise God for my Christian family. People sometimes ask how I landed at my home congregation of the Church of Christ in Plano, Texas. I've told many people, "I think it's because God had a place for me there." When we left West Texas, we intended to live in Grapevine, Texas, but that didn't work out. This did. I was convinced that the time and the place were right. And maybe, just maybe, I was meant to help the congregation through a very bleak time, after which we would be led by God-fearing, God-following shepherds, for whom I thank the Lord.

I've poured my heart out to you in this chapter. When I said that I would be bearing my soul, I meant it.

Each time we are tempted to focus on the negative, we need to remember God's promises to us. Before we close, let's concentrate on the blessings He freely gives us. The Bible is full of God's promises, but here are just a few:

- "…What is impossible with men is possible with God" (Luke 18:27).

- "…I will give you rest" (Matthew 11:28).

- "For God so loved the world…" (John 3:16).

- "My grace is sufficient for you…" (II Corinthians 12:9).

- "…He will make your paths straight" (Proverbs 3:6).

- "I can do everything through him who gives me strength." (Philippians 4:13).

- "…God works for the good of those who love him…" (Romans 8:28).

- "…He is faithful and just and will forgive us our sins…" (1 John 1:9).

- "…God will meet all your needs…" (Philippians 4:19).

- "God did not give us a spirit of timidity…" (II Timothy 1:7).

- "Cast all your anxiety on him because he cares for you." (1 Peter 5:7).

- "…You are in Christ Jesus, who has become for us wisdom from God…" (1 Corinthians 1:30).

- "…Never will I leave you; never will I forsake you" (Hebrews 13:5).

God is in control.

nine
Love is

Do you remember the scene that used to await people when they got off an airplane? A sea of people were always there waiting for their loved ones at the gate. Faces used to light up with smiles as each person spotted a loved one. The traveler might have been gone a day or a year, but you always saw love, companionship, and fellowship. Unfortunately, since 9/11, security issues don't allow that anymore. I don't know about you, but I miss those days.

Between my junior and senior years in high school, I had the opportunity to go to Brazil for six weeks on a youth exchange program. Family members came to the airport to send me off. When I returned six weeks later, those same family members were there to welcome me home. The hugs and relationships we used to see right at the gate are now limited to outside the secure areas.

I am a "touchy-feely" person. When I shake your hand, I like to put my other hand on your elbow or shoulder. I enjoy hugs. We've talked about the importance of touch and how crucial it is to feel loved. Our relationships include at least three types of love: emotional, physical, and spiritual. The more we care for one another, the more we're able to feel for one another, help one another and understand what each other is going through. If we have no real relationship, we tend to take a hands-off approach.

We might say, "Well, I know he's having trouble, but he'll get through it." But if we have a great relationship with someone, we go through the ups and downs of life right along with that person. That relationship is a part of us.

Maybe you've seen the cell phone commercial where a dad comes in and gives each of his two daughters a new cell phone. They seem excited, and he says; "Now we can talk as much as we want to." They just stare at him.

The mom is standing behind him, and she adds, "And you can talk to your friends all you want to, too."

The girls say, "Oh, that's great!" Then they give their mom a big hug.

The dad reaches for his wife and daughters and says, "Group hug." Their response is to look at him and then all three of them turn and walk away. And he's left standing there all alone. I guess that commercial is meant to be funny, but it kills me. I don't enjoy that advertisement at all, because it represents someone who really cares yet is rejected. Have you ever been in that situation and wondered why you were rejected? Have you ever felt as if true love was not there?

THE PORTRAIT OF TRUE LOVE

The movie *Love Story* made this line famous: "Love means never having to say you're sorry." For years, I didn't understand what that meant. When I think about it now, to me it means that I should never do anything to others that would require me to apologize to them. And that's a perfect world, right? We can't achieve perfection in our relationships, but I think it's a goal we should strive for. True love is to seek one another's higher good. If we do that, we probably won't need to apologize very often.

In 1 Corinthians 13:4–8, one of the best-known passages in the Bible, Paul paints the portrait of true love:

> Love is patient, love is kind. It does not envy, it does not boast, it is not proud. It is not rude, it is not self-seeking, it is not easily angered, it keeps no record of wrongs. Love does not delight in evil but rejoices with the truth. It always protects, always trusts, always hopes, always perseveres. Love never fails…

I John 2:9 basically says that if we don't love others—if we don't love as Jesus loved—we can't be brothers and sisters of Christ. There's not a thing in the world I wouldn't do for my family. Would I give my life for them? Certainly, no questions asked. Now, if I'm asked to sacrifice myself for someone else, I'm going to consider the cost. For instance, if sacrificing myself was the only way to save my Christian family, I could probably do that. Let's take it one step further. What if I were asked to sacrifice my wife or children for others? Well, that's a different story. Doing that would be a lot more difficult, because the love I have for my family is even greater than the love I have for myself.

Matthew 22:37 tells us, "…Love the Lord your God with all your heart and with all your soul and with all your mind." Verse 39 goes on to say, "…Love your neighbor as yourself." I can probably love my neighbor as myself, but it's another thing for me to love my neighbor as much as I love my family. God calls us to a higher level of loving than many of us are mature enough to handle. The love that God asks of us demands that we love everyone more than ourselves and that takes growth. We can only obtain that love through truly experiencing God's love.

One of my favorite photos is of me as a young man lying on the couch. What makes it special is that my daughter, Miranda, is lying on my chest. She's just an infant, but on her face is the purest expression of love. Peace and love are evident in her eyes as she cuddles with me, her father. It's a touching picture.

We've talked before about the passage in Matthew 18 where Jesus tells the disciples that unless they become like little children, they cannot inherit the kingdom of God. We should all have that look of wonder, love, trust, and amazement as we lie on our Father's chest and enjoy the comfort and security He gives us. We should allow ourselves to go there. We are God's children and, as such, we can put our full trust, hope, and love in Him.

No children should ever have to doubt whether their father would take care of them at all costs. I'm not a big guy, but if somebody crosses one of my kids, the hair stands up on the back of my neck. I'm going to do everything possible to defend my children, and they've always known that. Now, does that mean I did not discipline my kids? Certainly not, because that, too, is part of love.

While considering our relationship with our heavenly Father, and trying to relate it to the relationship between children and their fathers, I'm reminded of the old movie *Follow Me, Boys!* I love that film. Even as a kid, it made me cry. In the film, one boy carries a tough exterior, but deep inside, he needs others to reach out to him. His dad is an alcoholic and his addiction takes him away from his son on an emotional level. In an effort to reach out to his son, the father attended a party one evening. If I remember correctly the party was given for the Boy Scout troop that his son was a part of. The father shows up late...and drunk, and he is carrying a carton of melted ice cream. The boy is embarrassed to see his father, and wishes he had not shown up. Ah, man, that scene just tears my heart out.

Have you ever wished you had a different father or mother? Have you ever said, "I wish my dad was like so-and-so"? I have to admit that I have. There was a time in my life when I was embarrassed by my dad. He has always been the life of the party, and everyone says he looks and sounds just like Ross Perot.

One time, my dad and I were at a father/son outing on the Llano River. You could hear my dad having a good time from a long way away. His voice was echoing off the cliffs, and some of my friends were laughing at him. I was embarrassed. I now realize I have the most amazing dad in the world, and I would not trade him for anything. He has forgiven me for that instance of being ashamed of him, and I pray he's forgotten it.

Have you ever been there? Have you ever looked back and realized that you denied the Father? Peter did it. He denied the Son and, in doing so, he denied the Father. (see Matthew 26:69–75) How many times in my Christian walk have I done that as well? But do you know what? The love of the Father is forgiving. He knows I've denied

Him and been embarrassed to be called His child at times. There have been occasions when I didn't feel comfortable with someone knowing whose name I wore. Why is that? It was weakness. I needed to mature and, thank God, I have. When you think about it, isn't denying the heavenly Father a worse offense than denying our earthly father?

THE MANY ASPECTS OF LOVE

My wife and I kept our little granddaughter, Mary Alice, one weekend. She was barely talking and certainly not to the point that we could carry on a conversation with her. She was only saying a few words, but she had some CDs based on Scripture that she loved listening to. One of them was centered on 1 Corinthians 13. As she was getting ready for bed, she started singing for all she was worth, "Love is patient. Love is kind. I Corinthians 13:4 says, 'Love is patient and kind.'" She sang this over and over and over. I bet she sang that song twenty times. Of course, we thought it was cute, but we were also thankful she was learning that virtue at such a young age. We need to think about how we can sing that virtue into our lives.

I Corinthians 13 has always been referred to as the "love chapter" of the Bible. It gives us the real characteristics of godly love. So, let's examine the many aspects of love based on this well-known passage. For some of the points, I'll share personal stories. For others, I think the Word of God speaks loud and clear. Perhaps your life will provide a fitting story.

Love Is Patient

My sweet wife has been waiting on me to finish every meal we've eaten together for the last thirty years. I am a slow eater. In fact, I'm always the last one in my family to finish eating, no matter where we are. Even my grandkids wait on Grumpy (that's where I got the name). Love is patient, so they wait. There's no reason to get short about things like that.

Be patient. This idea goes back to the first chapter we covered on being still. Be still, understand, take in the aroma, and enjoy the togetherness. I have had to work hard to improve my patience. My fuse used to be extremely short, but it has gotten better as I've grown older. There's definitely some wisdom to be gained as you mature. Take the time to be patient with your children.

Now, showing patience and love to your children doesn't mean you are totally tolerant with them. It certainly doesn't mean overlooking bad behaviors, even when they're funny.

Love Is Kind

Have you ever practiced kindness toward people until it became a habit? Perhaps you've said something like, "Look, I don't really like that person. He's not someone I'd choose to vacation with. But I need to love him and get to know him because he needs my help." So, you start spending time getting to know him. And guess what? The next thing you know, you've developed love for that person. A great way to do this is to look for an opportunity to serve alongside someone. You will begin to feel a fellowship that comes from serving the Lord together.

Bruce Bennett is one of the best friends I have ever had in this world. We enjoyed great times together raising our families in Denver City. I really got to know Bruce when he and I went to Plains, Texas, on Sunday afternoons to study the Bible with the jail inmates. We rode there together every week and were locked in a jail cell for an hour at a time. When you do that, you get to know your brother. Because we were serving together, our love and friendship grew.

Love Does Not Boast

Boasting is not what love is about. It's not for getting pats on the back. Sometimes boasting can take the form of forcing others to look at all of our vacation photos. Just a handful is all they need to see. No one likes to listen to others toot their own horn.

In my real estate office, there is one lady who always has to outdo everyone else. If anyone tells a story about a child or grandchild, she's got to tell one about hers. Her tales are always bigger, better, and grander than anybody else's. Do you know someone like that? That's not what love is. Love listens, because that's what people need. Just listen.

Love Is Not Proud

Have you ever thought about that? I've thought about it many times. God gave me the gift of my wife, and I'm the last person who deserved her. And after He gave me Paula, He gave me two kids I certainly don't deserve. They have grown up in spite of me to become faithful Christians and responsible people. I remember some of the things I did as they were growing up and can't help but wonder how they turned out so well. I did some things right, too, but it was because I looked to God, who had a great hand in helping me raise my kids.

A few years ago, I wrote about twenty-five short stories on people and events that have touched my life. One I titled "Two Things I Noticed." The story was about how I saw Paula one September at the Adventures in Missions program in Lubbock, Texas, before I actually met her the following February. When I saw her, I knew I wanted to get to know her.

There were two things I noticed about Paula. The first was her beauty. There was something about her that made me say, "Wow!" I thought, *Man, she's special, and I want to get to know her.* This was before I knew her name or anything else about her. I figured out from the group she hung out with that she must have been from the Sunset Church of Christ in Lubbock. I was going to be back in Lubbock a few months later, so I set a goal of trying to meet her.

Well, I got my wish. Paula and I officially met and began to get to know each other. I lived with my Aunt Linda and Uncle Derrell and their two children while I was in the Adventures in Missions program. Whenever I had Bible study sessions with my uncle, Paula would come over to babysit my little cousins. I couldn't help but notice how lovingly she interacted with the children. I thought to myself, *She's going to be an amazing mother.* That was the second thing I noticed about her. She lovingly served. Paula was not too proud to serve by sitting with kids she didn't know so a man she barely knew could teach his uncle about Jesus. Love was instilled in me because of her actions, and it has been passed on to our children.

Love Is Not Self-Seeking or Easily Angered

Here's another "Grump-ism" for you, "you can't unsmush bread." Have you ever thought about that? I hate it when I bring home a loaf of bread and find it mashed. It's just not the same as it was before. Even if you try to unsmush it, you can never get it back in the same shape it was in.

It's also difficult to unsmush relationships. Even though we know we need to forgive, how many of us leave the handle of the hatchet sticking out of the ground? It's always there. But love tells us to bury the hatchet. It tells us that we can unsmush relationships.

Have you made it there? In your relationships, when someone flies off the handle with you or says something to hurt your feelings, are you ever able to forget it? If you can, praise God. I thank you for your spiritual maturity. I pray that I can get there someday. I work on it, but it's hard. And it goes both ways. Have you ever let a phrase pass your lips and then said, "Why in the world did I say that?" You realized that you just smushed bread and stepped on someone's feelings. No matter how hard you apologize, you can never take back what you said.

Love keeps a short fuse away from open flames. Don't let a short fuse or stinging tongue get in the way of a good relationship.

Love Does Not Keep Score

We are called to build trust by being honest in all our actions. If your spouse has ever lied to you, how hard is it to trust him or her again? If your business partner has ever cheated you, how tough is it to trust that person again? Think about this: we have all lied to and cheated on God. The good news is that if we repent and ask for forgiveness, God doesn't remember it. When sin is taken out of God's book, it doesn't exist anymore. It's not on the page. He doesn't remember it; only we do. That's where peace comes in. That's when we're able to forgive ourselves because God has already forgiven us.

Love Always Protects, Trusts, and Hopes

We sometimes say, "Love is blind." Wouldn't it be nice if that motto were completely true? Love does cover a multitude of sins and faults, and if we really love each other, we can overlook shortcomings in one another. That's the way relationships are supposed to work. And, brothers and sisters, we need to let that work not only in our married lives but also in our spiritual lives. We need to overlook one another's shortcomings.

Allow me to give a farmer's view of protection, trust, and hope. The quickest way to see protection in action is to make a newborn pig squeal. You will be amazed at the swiftness of a three hundred pound sow as she comes to defend one of her own. Trust is demonstrated several times a day by that mongrel of a mutt that has become the family pet. He will follow you anywhere you go because of his belief in you. Finally the hope of the farmer is unparalleled as he sows the seed in the spring, in expectation of the harvest in the fall.

The love of God, demonstrated through us, protects at all cost. It trusts in God and the love of our brothers and sisters. It hopes for eternal salvation, not only for oneself, but also for all mankind.

LOVE DEMANDS ACTION

I believe that some parents today are afraid to let their children fail. They will do anything they can, no matter the cost, to make sure their kids are happy. Have you noticed that in our society? You can't fail children in schools today. You just don't do it, because it can hurt their self-esteem. But what happens when a child graduates and tries to find a job? Who is there to protect him or her? What are we teaching our future generations when we do not acknowledge that failure and wrong exist.

I believe we have a duty to God and society to teach our children that the world is not going to be laid at their feet. We have to teach our children that they are responsible for their own actions and that there are consequences for cheating, lying, and stealing. We need to teach them responsibility and that they have to do things on their own. Love is teaching. It is not complete tolerance. Love is taking the Word of God and correcting our children when they're in the wrong. Love is helping our children understand that they might face failure in this world. Love is showing our children the reality that they are not going to come in first place every time.

Most of us have grown up in a comfortable society. God has blessed us beyond belief, especially those of us who were born in the United States. Yet, there are many people who do not know God. We must emulate the love of Christ to those who do not have a personal relationship with Him. We must teach our children and grandchildren to develop a faith of their own so that they may continue to demonstrate the light and carry on the legacy we leave them. Let's instill strong Christian values in our youth by instructing them in the Word of God. Let's petition the Father that the Church of tomorrow will be strong and effective for Him. Let's pray that future generations might know God's love.

As you can tell from the last few paragraphs I feel very strongly about the need for parents to raise children of discipline and responsibility. I feel very strongly that we have a responsibility to live by faith and serve God. Now let's consider the words of Jesus from Matthew 25: 34–40:

Then the King will say to those on his right, "Come, you who are blessed by my Father; take your inheritance, the kingdom prepared for you since the creation of the world. For I was hungry and you gave me something to eat, I was thirsty and you gave me something to drink, I was a stranger and you invited me in, I needed clothes and you clothed me, I was sick and you looked after me, I was in prison and you came to visit me." Then the righteous will answer him, "LORD, when did we see you hungry and feed you, or thirsty and give you something to drink? When did we see you a stranger and invite you in, or needing clothes and clothe you? When did we see you sick or in prison and go to visit you?" The King will reply, "I tell you the truth, whatever you did for one of the least of these brothers of mine, you did for me."

Love demands action.

JUST LIKe me? Ten

It is a proven fact that children are greatly influenced by their parents. Parents have the responsibility to be the prime example in a child's life. I've seen parents who were perfect role models for their kids. I've seen some who were a negative influence. And, I have also seen parents who weren't an influence at all on their children.

When I began thinking about the influence parents have on their children, the song "Cat's in the Cradle" came to mind. You've probably heard this song about the father who never has time for his son, but the son wants to grow up to be just like his father. After the son has grown up, and the father finally decides he wants to spend time with him, the son is too busy. It's at this point the father realizes his son did grow up to be just like him. The song carries a profound message about how relationships often take a back seat to everyday life. Unfortunately, that's a reality for many families.

As the song explains, it can bring despair to an earthly father when he realizes his son has become just like him. In a different relationship, the same realization can bring a sense of unbelievable joy. In this chapter, we're going to explore how sons are like their fathers and how fathers are like their sons at times.

TESTING THE WATERS

If I were just like my son, who is now grown, I would be a much better father, husband, Christian, and friend. There have been periods in my life when I was just like Josh, although it wasn't a good thing. To illustrate this point, I will go all the way back to his infancy. Before I take you there, I want to look at Romans 7:15–25:

> I do not understand what I do. For what I want to do I do not do, but what I hate I do. And if I do what I do not want to do, I agree that the law is good. As it is, it is no longer I myself who do it, but it is sin living in me. I know that nothing good lives in me, that is, in my sinful nature. For I have the desire to do what is good, but I cannot carry it out. For what I do is not the good I want to do; no, the evil I do not want to do—this I keep on doing. Now if I do what I do not want to do, it is no longer I who do it, but it is sin living in me that does it. So I find this law at work: When I want to do good, evil is right there with me. For in my inner being I delight in God's law; but I see another law at work in the members of my body, waging war against the law of my mind and making me a prisoner of the law of sin at work within my members. What a wretched man I am! Who will rescue me from this body of death? Thanks be to God—through Jesus Christ our Lord! So then, I myself in my mind am a slave to God's law, but in the sinful nature a slave to the law of sin.

Earlier in the same chapter, Paul essentially says he didn't understand what sin was until the law identified sin for him. He didn't understand what was wrong with some of the things he was doing until the law told him that these things were wrong.

Go back to the very first sin. God laid down the law to Adam and Eve. He said, "Don't eat the fruit of the tree of the knowledge of good and evil," (see Genesis 2:16–17). Then the serpent came along and enticed them. Suddenly, they didn't understand what could possibly be wrong with eating the fruit. There it is, the first human inclination to do what we're told we're not supposed to do. For some reason, many of us have to find out the hard way. It seems to be human nature, in children as well as adults, to try and figure out why we're not supposed to do what we're told to avoid. We even test the waters to find out how close we can get to temptations without them hurting us.

Paul had a problem with that. Let's face it: Paul was a number one. He claimed to be the Jew of Jews (see Philippians 3:5). He was good at that. Then, as a Christian, he says, "I am the chief of sinners. I am the number one sinner" (see 1 Timothy 1:15–16). He knew he didn't deserve the forgiveness of God. He didn't deserve the salvation he had obtained.

In Romans, Paul was writing to Gentiles, so we have a group of people who weren't familiar with the old law. I like to picture the recipients of Paul's letter as a group of believers who were simply looking at God's will for them in light of what Christ did for mankind. The law of sin and death was the old law put away by the cross of Jesus, so

Christians live under the new law, which focuses on how to live for Him.

So what do we have to do to live for Him? We have to set our minds on the things God wants and not on what we want. In my own life, I have had to learn not to misinterpret my will as God's will. Sometimes I have been like a stubborn child, so busy trying to make God give me what I want that I haven't lived the Father's will.

SOMEONE'S HERO

Now, let's take a deeper look at father/child relationships. In my opinion, everyone is somebody's hero. No matter how great or unworthy you think you are, there's somebody looking up to you. Either way, you can use your influence for good or bad.

I remember when it came to my son's attention that everyone is somebody's hero. Josh played on the high school varsity football team, and they were gearing up for a pep rally. Due to league limitations on how many events a particular school could host, the pep rally was held at the elementary school instead of the high school. Everyone gathered in the gymnasium, and the cheerleaders and band started leading the crowd in the Mustang fight song. Then the football players came in sporting their jerseys and carrying their helmets. The elementary students, kindergarten through third grade, were enthralled by all the excitement.

After the rally, the football players walked by the elementary kids, and Josh was asked for his autograph. Can you imagine a junior in high school being asked for his autograph? He came home and said, "Dad, I never thought about those little kids looking up to me."

Josh was their hero. He was one of the Mighty Mustangs. Those little children aspired to be him one day. In the same way, someone is looking at us and aspiring to be what we are. We need to realize that.

How many of us followed in either of our parents' footsteps when choosing a career? We observe our parents and sometimes follow suit because of their influence. I was a farmer previously, and my son worked on the farm as he was growing up. I remember the first few times I told him to help with the hoeing. He just sat there moaning and groaning about how bad it was. Today, he's a dentist. But if you asked him what he would do if he could do anything he wanted, he'd say, "I'd move to West Texas and be a cotton farmer."

Why? Because he learned about life on a farm as he grew up, and now he can look back and appreciate it. He saw me do it, and he saw what kind of life I lived. It's humbling when I notice aspects of my son's life that reflect my own. Sometimes they're good, and I'm proud. Sometimes they're not so good, and I say, "Why did I teach him those things?" He's not perfect, and neither am I.

We need to make sure we're showing our kids the right attitudes and behaviors. How many of us miss Sunday night worship service to stay home and watch football? What message are we sending to our kids? What are we telling them about our priorities? As our children grow, we will see them take on many of our characteristics and priorities. It's amazing.

Parents sometimes follow their children's example as well. I've found myself reflecting my son at times, and I thank God for that. I've mentioned before that my son is a better man than I am, and Josh has taught me a lot in the past few years. When I was going through hard times, he talked to me man-to-man and even toe-to-toe on occasion. I remember one time when he was in high school and he came to me, saying, "Dad, what you're doing is wrong." How much intestinal fortitude does it take to stand up to your dad like that? Forget the fact he weighed a hundred-eighty pounds to my one hundred-thirty at the time. Still, how do you confront your dad and say, "That's not the way Christ would have you live"?

I had shown my son something was wrong in my life, and he was man enough to call me on it. I saw in him a part of me as my son and, at the same time, a part of him that was even stronger than me. Now I see myself reflecting him more and more because I realize that by doing so I can become a better man.

Of course, before he grew up to be such an outstanding young man, Paula and I had some interesting times with Josh. I'm now going to give you a few examples of how we as adults sometimes act as children—in a way that is contrary to God's will.

A CONTEST OF WILLS

Josh was a stubborn kid. When he was about eighteen months old, he was what you would call an extremely strong-willed child. One night, I was sitting in the living room while Paula and Josh were in the bathroom. Paula had just finished giving Josh a bath and had taken him out of the tub. For some reason, Josh opened a cabinet door. Paula asked him to close it, but he wouldn't. After a few more requests to close the door, I heard the first swat on his bare bottom, and Paula said, "Josh, close that door." Then I heard another swat, followed by, "Josh, close that door." For twenty minutes, I sat in the living room listening to her say, "Close the door, son." Swat.

At that point, I went into the bathroom. Josh was standing there naked. The more swats she gave, the more defiant he became. He glared at Paula with a look that said, "You are not going to make me do anything." His hands were tightened into fists, his jaw was clenched, he was gritting his teeth and there wasn't a tear in his eyes. For twenty more minutes, I stood at the door and watched as Paula continued to say, "Son, close that door." But he didn't close it. Why?

After forty minutes had passed, Paula looked at me and said, "Kent, I can't do this." I grabbed the boy by the shoulders and said, "Son, close that door." Josh looked at Paula, raised his head up, reached over and closed the door. Hard-headed? You bet. What started as a minor open-cabinet incident grew into a test of wills. Paula and

I admire strong will and determination, but we believe it must be channeled in the right direction.

Over the past few years, I've recognized myself as that eighteen-month-old kid on occasion. So many times the Father has told me, "Kent, you need to do it this way." But I tried to make my will, God's will. I butted my head against the door, saying, "I'm not going to do it Your way. I'm going to do it my way." I was willing to take the punishment of having no peace because I wanted to do it my way. Why?

Josh had a pretty short fuse as a little child. I'm sure he got that from me, because he saw me exhibit a short temper several times. He has worked on that, and now I'm watching him to learn how to lengthen my fuse. But there were times as a little child when he would walk by the rocking chair and accidentally bump his head. Well, he was of the mindset that the chair shouldn't have done that to him. We're talking about a kid who was barely walking. He would grab the arm of the rocking chair with both hands and bash his head into it. Boom! Boom! It's as if he was saying, "I told you!" He was punishing the chair.

I've looked at my life and considered the times I beat my head against my wife or parents' will because I was going to do what I wanted. But mostly, I'm guilty of beating my head against my Father's will. Just as Josh came to realize that when Mom or Dad told him to do something, he'd better do it, I'm learning that when I give up my ideas—when I stop trying to make my will God's and start trying to make God's will mine—life is a lot easier.

We sometimes obey only out of fear, but as we mature, we begin to obey out of respect and love.

I'm glad to say I had my son's love and respect through all of the hard times we had. And I believe my and Paula's discipline as parents helped him become the kind of man he is today. But you know what? All the talking and discipline in the world would not have been effective if we had not lived, to the best of our ability and with God's help, according to the values we were trying to teach him. No one's perfect, but children see how their parents live and grow up knowing what is truly important to their parents.

SHOWING SUPPORT IN ALL SITUATIONS

We talked about Paul's struggles to do the right thing in Romans 7. Now let's look at what Paul wrote in Philippians 4:4–9:

> Rejoice in the LORD always. I will say it again: Rejoice! Let your gentleness be evident to all. The LORD is near. Do not be anxious about anything, but in everything, by prayer and petition, with thanksgiving, present your requests to God. And the peace of God, which transcends all understanding, will guard your hearts and your minds in Christ Jesus. Finally, brothers, whatever is true, whatever is noble, whatever is right, whatever is pure, whatever is lovely, whatever is admirable—if anything is excellent or praiseworthy—think about such things. Whatever you have learned or received or heard

> from me, or seen in me—put it into practice. And
> the God of peace will be with you.

In the passage we looked at earlier from Romans 7, Paul was saying that he does things he doesn't want to do and knows he shouldn't do. Now he tells us in Philippians, "Whatever you see me doing, you do it as well." (see Philippians 4:9) Paul had become a slave to God's will. When we become slaves to God's will, it becomes easier for us to avoid the things we shouldn't do. When we allow God in our lives, positive changes become possible. And remember, God loves us even when we're not quite what we should be. God loved Paul even when he persecuted Christians. God loved Paul when he said, "I'm struggling with doing things I know I shouldn't do."

Josh's senior year in football started off with a bang. Three games into the season, the Mighty Mustangs were undefeated. We had the top defense in Class A through Class AAAAA. Josh was the strong safety for a defense that was allowing fewer yards, and fewer points, than any other team on the high plains of Texas. And he had a hand in every touchdown for the team. As quarter-back, he either threw or carried the ball across the line every time our Denver City team scored for those first three games. Coaches from opposing Texas teams in the Lubbock, Odessa and San Angelo areas were quoted in their respective newspapers as saying, "We've got to watch out for number 18, Josh Smith. He's had a hand in every touchdown the Mustangs have had all season."

Josh's grandmother, Paula's mom, made a blanket sporting the Mustang colors of red and gray that featured Josh's name and jersey number. I took the blanket with me to every game. It didn't matter that for the first three games of the season, it was about ninety-six degrees. Being the dad I was, I proudly displayed the blanket. I also went to neighboring towns to pick up their local papers so I could find out what others were saying about Josh.

The next game in Greenwood, Texas, didn't go so well. Josh threw three interceptions in the first half. He still had a hand in all of the scoring, but this time, it was for the other team. I never sat with the crowd in the stands when Josh was playing football, especially not when he was quarterback. If you want to be the parent of a football quarterback or a baseball pitcher, God bless you and give you strength, because those positions catch all the flak. It's tough to sit in the stands and watch when everything goes wrong. So, I would stand by myself to watch the games. But this particular night, two friends from the coffee shop joined me. By halftime, they decided to go home. That's how bad it was. My head was hanging.

The Mustangs rallied in the second half, but it was not enough to win the game. We experienced our first loss of the season that night. As I walked around the end of the field to my car, I spread out the blanket for all to see and walked through the middle of the Greenwood crowd. Josh was known by everyone on the opposing side as the quarterback who had handed them the victory. But in one of my son's lowest moments on the athletic field for Denver City, I made sure that he knew how proud I was of him and how pleased I was to be his father. I carried his name and jersey number with my head held high as I walked through that crowd.

Have you thought about the fact that God does that for us? When you and I struggle and call out, "God, it's Your will that I want, but I'm having a hard time!" there's God, holding up our name and number and saying, "It's all right."

A LESSON IN HUMILITY

As proud as I was that night, I became even more proud just a few days later. The following Wednesday night, Josh was called on to teach the high school class at our congregation. He taught a lesson on pride and used his recent experiences as examples. He told the class about the complimentary newspaper articles mentioning his name and all the great things the opposing teams' coaches were saying about him. He now realized that all the positive attention had given him a big ego. As he looked back, he could say, "You know what? God took me down. I was too proud, and I needed to learn a lesson."

It takes incredible maturity for a seventeen-year-old to tell his friends, "I had become conceited and proud of my position, and I needed this lesson." When I look back at my life, I realize it took me much longer than Josh to figure out that God needs to humble me on occasion.

I've realized that the failures I shared with you a couple of chapters back might have come into my life because I needed to be humbled. Even as I said, "We made a good crop this year," I had developed a pompous and selfish attitude, and God needed to take me down a notch. We need to accept and understand that God disciplines those He loves. We don't need to blame God for our failures. Josh didn't blame God for throwing the three interceptions that night. Josh ended up thanking God for bringing him back to earth so that he would be more of a team player and a better leader to his teammates who followed him on the field every Friday night.

Our sons and daughters are like us in so many ways. If we want them to be like God, we've got to be like God. Let's ask God to help us become more like Him so that we can provide a good example to our children. In many cases, the way we parent our children gives them their first impressions of God as a Father. Let's live in such a way that we would be proud for our children to be like us. We can, with God's help. We just need to ask Him for it.

Oh, to be like You, Father. As Paul tells us in 1 Corinthians 13:13, "And now these three remain: faith, hope and love. But the greatest of these is love."

eLeven
me, GIve UP
conTROL?

Our culture encourages us to adopt the mentality of "me first," and "I'm in control," and "I'm the one in charge of this situation." Looking back on my life, I've subscribed to that way of thinking quite a bit. I didn't get the nickname "Little Caesar" for nothing—I earned it. People in my line of work knew that I was in charge, and that's just the way it was. Have you struggled with that as well? What makes us strive to always be in control?

To begin, let's look at Proverbs 3:5–6:

> Trust in the LORD with all your heart and lean not on your own understanding; in all your ways acknowledge him, and he will make your paths straight.

This has been one of my favorite passages for a long time, even though I haven't adhered to it as much as I should (after all, I'm a guy who likes to be in control). It's difficult for me, because most of the time I think my understanding is pretty good. But I have to realize that my understanding isn't what the Lord's is.

Proverbs is full of references to wisdom and the benefits of seeking and gaining this virtue. In a sense, we have to give up control to even gain wisdom. As we've discussed before, maybe we need to give up what we want to do in order to fit the pursuit of wisdom into our schedules.

Whether it's daily Bible reading or setting aside time to pray every day, we have to make a concerted effort to seek out the wisdom of God.

Most of us don't find time for activities that are not on our schedules, so we need to set up appointments on our calendar for these spiritual disciplines. This method has worked well for my daily Bible reading. We can certainly have prayerful thoughts throughout the day, but we also need specific times reserved for communicating with our Father. Find out what works for you, and don't let anything get in the way.

On one of our mission trips to Honduras, we were all exhausted as we came back to our rooms after the first day of work. I lay down and started thanking God for the day we had, and the next thing you know, I woke up. I started thanking God again for the day we'd had, and a minute later, I woke up again. About the fourth time I woke up, I said, "God, You know what I mean. I'm going to sleep."

The next morning at breakfast, I told my companions, "Man, I got in my prayers last night, and that dog just didn't hunt." Each of the other guys chimed in, "Yeah, me too. About two words into my prayer, I caught myself nodding off." It happened to all of us. So, we need to set a time when we can pay specific attention to praying to God and ask Him to help us relinquish control.

We also need to get over ourselves and realize that God's plan is bigger than us. Jeremiah 10:23 goes along with this idea when it says, "I know, O Lord, that a man's life is not his own; it is not for man to direct his steps." Well, if it's not for us to direct our own steps, who will? Either God or

Satan. Whoever is in charge of our lives is going to direct those steps. We need to give up control to God.

TAKING FLIGHT

Growing up, I had always wanted to fly. In fact, when I turned nineteen, I was going to be in the Air Force until an Army recruiter told me, "You can't fly in the Air Force unless you have a college degree. But you can fly in the Army without a college degree." However, my plans changed. I found myself in Blackfoot, Idaho, visiting a missionary whom our home congregation supported. I've told you about that before. The house I lived in was less than a half-mile from the airport. Every day, I heard airplanes taking off and landing, and I realized maybe I could still fulfill my dream to fly after all. I called my dad and said, "The airport is right in my backyard, and I'd really like to learn to fly."

He said, "Well, son, go to it. It's up to you. You got the money?"

"Yes, sir, I've got the money."

So I drove to the airport, walked in, and said, "I'm Kent Smith, and I want to learn how to fly."

The flight instructor, Pete, was chomping at the bit. That was how he made his living, so he said, "When do you want to start?"

"Man, I'm here," I said.

"All right," he replied. He took me out to an airplane and gave me an orientation on the basics. Then he said, "Crawl up on that wing, and get in on the left side."

So I climbed into the pilot's seat, and he joined me as copilot. He told me, "We're going to taxi now. You don't steer with the wheel; you steer with your feet." We taxied and lined up on the runway. He checked all the controls and said, "Now, I just want you to put your hands on the wheel and your feet on the pedals and leave them there as we take off."

"All right," I said. "That's great!"

So Pete gave it the gas, and we took off. We got about fifty feet off the runway when he said, "You're in control."

"What?" I asked.

"You're in control,"

I looked over at Pete. His hands weren't on the wheel, and his feet weren't on the pedals. I was flying that airplane! I was truly living my dream. It was amazing. We flew over the countryside and enjoyed a magnificent view from eight thousand feet. Then Pete told me how to stall an airplane on purpose. I couldn't help but ask, "Why would you want to do that?"

"Well," he said, "because you have to learn how to handle it when you get in those situations." And then he talked to me about the importance of altitude, which we discussed in a previous chapter.

As we started flying back to the airport, Pete said, "I'm going to take over now, but leave your hands on the wheel and your feet on the pedals. I'm going to let you feel this as we land the plane." We came in for the landing. Oh, man, that was sweet! I felt I was in control, but I really wasn't. Pete had the controls, but I was allowed to feel the experience.

When I had first climbed into that airplane, Pete didn't say, "Okay, start it up, and let's go." He didn't tell me to line it up on the runway, shoot the gas to it and just see what happened. He was in charge of the situation. He had the controls set so the plane would fly whether I had my hands on the wheel or not, and he knew we were going to be safe. He was in control.

In the same way, we need to allow Jesus to be in control as He's teaching us to live as Christians. Sometimes we feel like we're on top of a mountain, and sometimes we feel like our lives are in danger. But who is in control no matter what we experience in our lives? It's Jesus. He's the one at the controls. We have to learn to put our faith in Him.

Where would I have been without Pete's hands on the controls when we came in to land that day? It would have been a bad situation. Maybe I would have been lucky. Sometimes that's the way I fly my Christian life—blind. And you know what? I always end up crashing.

SOLO FLIGHT

I went to the airport for flying lessons as often as possible, and the time quickly came for my sixth session. So Pete and I went flying, and after only thirty minutes, he said, "Let's head back to the airport."

"Already?" I said.

"Yeah," he replied. "I got some stuff to do. Sorry to have to cut you short."

We flew back to the airport, touched down and taxied back to the hangar. Pete said, "All right. I'm getting out, but you take the plane out again. I'd like you to do three touch and go's."

It was solo time! After only five and a half hours of flying, I was about to be in control. I went to the end of the runway and checked the engine. I did everything I was supposed to do. My hands were sweating, and my concentration was unbelievable. Then I took off. I climbed to about two thousand feet and began my left hand pattern for a landing; I handled the radio and set the flaps. I approached the runway. The wheels touched down, and I shot the gas to it. I lifted off again and exclaimed, "Yaaaaah!" Exhilaration! I was in control of this airplane by myself. I was the one who took off and landed without any help from anybody. Now, it's true I had learned a few things from the instructor, but man, this was great! I was in control!

I went through the routine two more times and then stopped and walked into the flight instructor's office. "All right," Pete said, "Let's cut off the shirttail."

It's a tradition for a pilot in training to cut off his or her shirttail after the first successful solo flight. You know what? I'd worn a shirt without a tail. I'd worn a pullover shirt with elastic around the waist because I had no idea I was going to solo that day. So instead of a shirttail, I might be the only person in the history of aviation to hang a pair of socks on the flight school's bulletin board. That's okay. I was excited because I had accomplished something I had always wanted to do.

TOO MUCH FUN

Maybe you've heard the country song "I Ain't Never Had Too Much Fun." Well, I found out it is possible to have too much fun. When I went to the airport for the first time and experienced my first flying lesson, I told Pete he couldn't teach me fast enough. He said, "All right, that's what I like to hear." He handed me some books and said, "Now, you study these things."

I agreed and went to flight lessons every other day. Not even two weeks had passed from the time of my first flight lesson to that of my first solo flight. I was getting my time in. After a couple of solo flights, Pete said, "We're going on a cross country flight." So we headed out, "Set your VOR to thus and such." (VOR is a type of radio navigation system for aircraft.)

"My what?" I asked.

"Set your VOR,"

"What's a VOR?"

"Haven't you been studying your books?"

"Well, you know, I've been having so much fun flying that I haven't read my books yet." I wasn't paying attention to the rules or what I was supposed to do. So, we started our Idaho cross-country flight from Blackfoot to Arco. From there, we headed down to American Falls. From American Falls, we went back up to our starting point in Blackfoot. It was a great trip, and everything went smoothly.

When we landed back in Blackfoot, Pete asked, "You got time to come back this afternoon?"

"Oh, yeah," I said. "I'm all for it."

"Okay, this afternoon you're going to make that same flight yourself. It's time for your first solo cross-country flight."

"All right," I replied, "I'm ready!"

I ate lunch and went back to the airport. I took off for Arco and then headed toward American Falls. The VOR station was at the American Falls airport. After I had been flying along for a while, I started feeling like I should have already arrived.

I called the tower at American Falls, and the air traffic controller said, "Where are you coming from?"

"Arco," I said. "I'm on my solo cross country."

"That's great," the air traffic controller replied. "The VOR station is right at the runway. Come on in."

"Okay." So, I kept on going. When more time passed and I still wasn't there, I called back in.

The guy gave me the same information again and said, "We're right here."

I kept flying with no luck. The third time I called in, the air traffic controller said, "Tell you what. I think when you get here, you need to visit with the flight instructor."

When I finally arrived, I found the flight instructor and said, "I'm Kent Smith, and I'm on my solo cross country."

"Where did you come from?" he asked.

"I left Blackfoot, went to Arco, and then turned and came down here,"

"What? You went from Blackfoot to Arco to here?"

"Yeah,"

"What kind of nut is teaching you how to fly that airplane?"

"Well, I don't know. Until just now, I thought he was okay."

"Rattlesnakes can't even live where you've been," the flight instructor said. "It's a lava bed, and there's not a smooth spot to land for miles. I can't believe he sent you out there. Have you heard of the Snake River?"

"Yes sir."

"Well, the Snake River comes from Idaho Falls, goes through Blackfoot down to Pocatello and then over here to American Falls. When you take off, find the Snake River. You can't miss it. Follow it back to Blackfoot. When you land there, tell your instructor you need more training."

"Yes, sir," I said. "I believe I do." So I followed the Snake River back to Blackfoot and landed. From that time on, I stopped having too much fun and got serious about studying my flight books. I realized that day that being in control can be a dangerous situation if you don't know how to handle what you're controlling.

How many times have we thought we were in control when, all of a sudden, we realized we weren't? When I came to the realization that I was lost and couldn't pick myself up by my own bootstraps, I had to ask somebody else to be in control. I had to ask God to do what I couldn't do and save me from failure. I had been having too much fun flying, and I needed an instructor to put me in my place. While having too much fun, I hadn't realized what a dangerous situation I had put myself in and how it could have ended with tragic results.

We can also experience disaster by trying to control our lives instead of handing that control to Christ. We need to tell Jesus, "It's time for You to take control, because I've been having too much fun. I've lost control, and I need to turn around. I need to lean on You and hand these reins back to You because I've made a mess of my life."

SOME THINGS ARE BIGGER THAN US

I've told you briefly about a plane crash I had several years ago. Our former congregation in Denver City, Texas, hosts the Teenage Christian Conference every year. One particular year, the preacher, Jeff Walling, was scheduled to speak and needed transportation to his next destination. So I got my airplane ready. Right after Jeff's talk, we headed for the airplane.

A friend of mine, who was also a pilot, was in front with me, and Jeff was in the back. As we took off, the plane didn't feel right and we had trouble gaining altitude. In spite of my best efforts, our plane clipped a power line and we started falling. "Well, boys," I said, "we're going down." Amazingly, I was calm, cool, and collected. I don't know how I was able to do that. In that moment of impending disaster, I said, "Lord, please take care of us." It's times like these when we realize we're in dire need. We are most sincere about surrendering to God when we're reaching out for something to hold on to.

When's the last time you called out to the Lord because you knew you were out of control? When's the last time you said to God, "In this life and death situation, please rescue me from the pit. Get me safely to the ground." That day in the plane, God delivered us from what could have been a catastrophe. All three of us walked away from the crash. Sore? Yes. Bruised? Yes. My confidence was also bruised, but you know what? I had been humbled. Sometimes in our Christian walk, we need to learn to put aside self-confidence and humble ourselves before God. When we sing the song "All to Jesus I Surrender," do we truly embrace the meaning in our hearts?

You've probably heard someone say, "That guy is a picture of success. He has everything going for him. He's tall, dark, and handsome." Remind you of King Saul? He was head and shoulders above the rest, and his physical presence demanded that others take him seriously (see 1 Samuel 9:2). He clearly looked the part of a king. On the other hand, if you were to describe me, you'd say I am short, pale, and kind of cute. So, I've never been anyone's picture of success.

Take Jesus as another example. Scripture tells us in Isaiah 53:2 that "…He had no beauty or majesty to attract us to him, nothing in his appearance that we should desire him." But you know what? It doesn't matter who we are or how the world perceives us. We can lose everything we have in an instant. We may think we are in control, but we are not.

Sometimes I dream about being on a 747 when the pilot has a heart attack and someone's got to take over the plane. Who's it going to be? I think, *I'm a pilot! I'll do it!* It's fun to think about, but, in reality, I would be in over my head. It's been about fifteen years since I've piloted an airplane. I do believe I could go to the airport tomorrow morning, get in a Piper aircraft, take off, fly around, land it, and be just fine. I wouldn't be frightened to do that, but I know I'm not ready to fly a jumbo jet.

Sometimes we need to evaluate our level of maturity in our Christian walk. There are reasons sheep need a shepherd. Sheep are basically dumb. A group of sheep will get so close together in a storm that they bury their noses in each other's fleece and smother themselves to death. We are a lot like sheep. We sometimes make dumb decisions and are prone to blindly follow the crowd. God knows all this because He created sheep, and He created us. We all need a shepherd to give us spiritual leadership.

Folks, this Christian walk is bigger than we are, and we cannot do it without God's help. We cannot do it without the help of one another. We cannot pull this load alone, no matter how much we want to. We all need help. It's just like me learning to be humble when it comes to flying. Even though I can fly a Cessna 150, I realize I can't fly a 747 or Lear jet. There are things that are bigger than us, and we don't have all the answers.

"LORD, TAKE CONTROL"

Another time when we were in Honduras, I was helping with our medical mission efforts. Remember when we talked in the first chapter about being still and how movement and noise can distract us? That idea became clear to us in this situation, because our setup was such that the crowds were in the same room with us. The dentists were pulling teeth, and we only had sheets to separate the patients and us from the waiting crowd. The setting was noisy and chaotic.

We didn't realize the effect the first day's crowd had on us until the second day when we moved to a school building that was only large enough for the patients and us. Everyone else waited outside. I asked, "Boys, you all hear that?"

"Hear what?" they asked.

"That's my point," I said. "I don't know about you all, but I'm more relaxed today." Everyone agreed that it was much quieter. The moment was so peaceful I started singing one of my favorite songs, "Lord, Take Control," which is the theme of this chapter. It talks about giving our hearts, minds, bodies, and souls to God and offering ourselves as living sacrifices. I hope the next time you hear that song; it will carry special meaning for you in light of what we've considered in this chapter.

Lord, take control. May that always be our prayer.

TWeLve
TRUSTING in
THe LORD

Has anything or anyone ever caused you to stop and think? I pray this chapter will help you do just that. The principles we have talked about in the last eleven chapters can be lived out in our lives by thinking about our relationship to God.

If we turn our focus to God, we can live a still life. We can become emotionally involved in our devotion to God and overcome a stagnate existence of repetition and tradition. We can come to realize that God is standing beside us and that where He is present is holy ground. We can desire to serve as Jesus served. We can stand with courage among the family of God and be comforted by the fact that we are never alone. We can live our lives transparently for the entire world to see and allow others to understand that there is nothing false in us. We can use our voices in praise to God. We can model a life of light to the world. We can know that failure is a growing process, and we can chose how we respond to it. We can be confident in the love of God and begin sharing that love with others. We can become like children in our pure dependence on God and turn away from childish defiance. We can ask God for help in giving up total control of our lives to Him.

In this chapter, we will discuss how we can more willingly trust in the Lord. And finally, in the last chapter, we will discuss how we can have the peace of a gently flowing river as we live our lives for God. James 4:8 tells us, "Come near to God and he will come near to you." We're going to take a look at six ways we can more fully trust in God. I think you'll find the Scriptures and stories related to each point encouraging to you as you apply these ideas to your life.

TRUST IN GOD'S TIMING

First, we have to learn to trust in God's timing. This one is often hard for us because we don't like to wait for anything. We live in an instant world, and we want everything right now.

I was in the supermarket one day and thought, *Man, I haven't had Cream of Wheat in a long time.* The store carried regular Cream of Wheat that could be cooked in a microwave in two and a half to three minutes. There was also an instant Cream of Wheat that could be cooked in one to one and a half minutes. Now, which one do you think I bought? The instant variety, of course…I want it now.

My wife and I bought a coffee pot with a timer a while back. We set the timer at night, and when we get up in the morning, there is no waiting for the coffee to brew. We want it right now. No wonder we don't understand God's timing, what He has in store for us, and why we can't have what we want right now.

At times, I've been impatient about some of the events in my life and said, "Lord, let's turn this thing around." I believed I was being disciplined and that maybe I needed to learn to humble myself, but I was still in a hurry. I wanted an instant turnaround, not a long-term turnaround. We need to trust in God's timing.

I'd like us to take a look at Psalm 104. This whole Psalm is relevant to our topic, but it's too lengthy to include here. However, I recommend you take the time to read the entire chapter. For now, I'll just share one verse in particular that jumps out at me. Psalm 104:24 say, "How many are your works, O Lord! In wisdom you made them all; the earth is full of your creatures."

This psalm talks about the greatness and glory of God in creating the heavens and the earth. It mentions how the water was on the face of the earth and how the waters disappeared into their own place at the sound of God's voice and went where He told them they could go. It talks about the animals God created and the way in which they succumb to Him. It relates how He gave breath to the animals and how, at His word, that breath can be taken away. We may not understand His plan, but the Word says He feeds all those that are His in His own time.

Maybe you remember the song "Turn! Turn! Turn! (To Everything There Is a Season)," which was made popular by The Byrds in 1965. It's actually based on Ecclesiastes 3, another passage of Scripture that is best read in its entirety. It's poignant, and the meaning is sometimes hard to accept. It states there is a time for everything God has planned in our lives. We just don't always understand that timing.

I have a close friend named Ken McLeroy who lives in Denver City. I met Ken and his family when they came to the congregation we used to attend in Denver City. It was more than twenty years ago, but I remember that day vividly because I preached the sermon before they came forward to place membership. Over the years, Ken and I became close.

Ken has a congenital heart defect. The doctors estimate his heart is functioning at about 10 percent of its capacity, and it's been that way for years. More than 10 years ago, Ken told me, "Kent, when I go, I want you to perform my funeral."

"Well, Ken, it would be my honor," I replied. "I don't know why I deserve such a privilege."

"Well, I want you to," he said, "so you just have to tell me you'll do it."

So, I promised I would. Several years later, I announced to our congregation, "Paula and I are moving to the Metroplex." After the service, I went to Ken and said, "Brother, this doesn't mean I'm leaving you."

"And it doesn't mean I'm letting you go. When I pass on, you're still going to do my funeral."

We visited Ken a couple of Christmas holidays ago. We thought it might be the last time we would see him. The next September, as I was getting ready to leave on another Honduras mission trip, I received a letter from Ken's wife, Daun. Ken's health wasn't good, and she was really down. So I called her. She said, "Kent, it's going to happen any time now."

"Well, Daun," I said, "I'm supposed to leave for Honduras, but I won't go if you think it's best."

"I've got to have you here, you know?"

I was torn over what to do, so I called the preacher Skip Rodgers, back in Denver City. Skip said, "Ken's had better days, but we think maybe Daun is just a little down right now. We don't know God's timing."

I decided to go ahead with the trip, and Daun started praying, "Father, You can't let Ken die while Kent's gone." I found out she had also prayed the same prayer when I went to Honduras the previous June.

Doctors can't explain how Ken's heart is still hanging on. Sometimes it pounds more than two hundred beats per minute even though it's operating with limited capacity. I don't know how Ken hangs on, except that God is the one in control of the time.

Talk about the life of a servant! That will be my message at his funeral. Ken McLeroy demonstrates more of a servant attitude than anyone I've ever met. In fact, if you visited his congregation this coming Sunday, if he were at all able, Ken would be serving coffee to everyone who walked into his Bible class. That's the kind of man he is. The time is up to God. God knows when Ken's work here is done. God knows that lives are being blessed as long as Ken's here, but He also knows that lives will continue to grow when Ken's gone. We don't have to understand God's timing; we just have to hold God's hand.

RELY ON GOD'S PROMISES

The second item we need to work on is to rely on God's promises. II Peter 1:1–8 has much to say about how we can learn to rely on Him:

> Simon Peter, a servant and apostle of Jesus Christ,
> To those who through the righteousness of our

God and Savior Jesus Christ have received a faith as precious as ours: Grace and peace be yours in abundance through the knowledge of God and of Jesus our Lord. His divine power has given us everything we need for life and godliness through our knowledge of him who called us by his own glory and goodness. Through these he has given us his very great and precious promises, so that through them you may participate in the divine nature and escape the corruption in the world caused by evil desires. For this very reason, make every effort to add to your faith goodness; and to goodness, knowledge; and to knowledge, self-control; and to self-control, perseverance; and to perseverance, godliness; and to godliness, brotherly kindness; and to brotherly kindness, love. For if you possess these qualities in increasing measure, they will keep you from being ineffective and unproductive in your knowledge of our Lord Jesus Christ.

Through what do we receive God's promises? Through His divine power. God has provided us with His glory, goodness, and knowledge. All we have to do is accept them in our hearts. If we let the Word live in our lives, He has promised that we are His children and that we will obtain eternal life. We have the promise that nothing is going to happen to us that we can't handle with God's help.

There is a plaque I look at every morning in my bathroom as I wash my face. It reads, "God, help me remember that nothing is going to happen today that You and I can't handle." How do I know that? Because He promised us. I Corinthians 10:13 basically says, "Look, I'm not going to give you anything except what is common to man and that you can overcome." God is not going to give us more than we can handle. We need to hear, understand and rely on promises such as this. If we rely on His promises when we are weak, they will remind us that God is there for us, and this will give us strength.

There's a song that more or less says, "When I'm at my lowest, I have to keep calling on Your name." And you know, that's what we need to do. When we're at our lowest, we have to keep calling on God. We don't need to get to the point where we say there is no use. We just need to remember that God promises to be with us. Even when He doesn't feel near, we have to understand that He is right there with us because He promised He would be.

Why are some days good and others bad? Why do some of us suffer and others don't? Why do bad things happen to good people? Why do bad people continue to get rich? You know what? It doesn't matter. Why? Because man isn't capable of comprehending the majesty of God and the work of His hand. All we can do is just continue to believe in Him and know that He has everything under control. So, we need to rely on the promises He gave us.

WAIT FOR GOD'S ANSWERS

Third, we've got to wait for God's answers. Now, this has a lot to do with trusting in God's timing, which we discussed earlier. We are an impatient lot. Paul asked for the thorn to be removed from his flesh three times. We are told in Luke 11 that if we knock on our neighbor's door and ask for bread, and he tells us to go away, we should continue to knock until he gives in and gives us bread.

The point is that if we boldly ask God, He is going to take care of us. God's response to Paul's request was that His grace was sufficient. I don't know what the thorn was, but I understand that God answered his prayer. It wasn't the way Paul wanted it answered, but the prayer was answered. And we know God answered it the way He did because He had a purpose in Paul's suffering.

There's a country western song Garth Brooks sings that indicates he is thankful for unanswered prayers." However, there's no such thing as an unanswered prayer. God sometimes tells us no, but that's still an answer. Just because God doesn't do for us what we think He should doesn't mean He isn't answering our requests. God knows what's best for us even when we don't.

How many of us have children who have asked for something we knew they didn't need? We as parents know better. When I was a teenager, I just about wore my mom out asking for a motorcycle. She was not a fan of my idea and continually told me, "Son, you're not going to get a motorcycle."

I still can't believe it, but I told her I had the money and I was going to buy a motorcycle. It wasn't long before I was riding that motorcycle to a hospital to visit one of my friends who had been in a motorcycle accident. On my way to the hospital, less than a mile from my house, I had to lay my motorcycle on the ground to keep from colliding with a car that turned in front of me.

Mom knew best. Mom knew it was to my advantage to not have that motorcycle, because she knew how uncoordinated I was. Sometimes we have the answers, but most of the time we don't. God always does. Let the answers come from God.

Here are a couple of passages that encourage us to wait on the Lord and be patient for His answers:

- Psalm 37:1–7: "Do not fret because of evil men or be envious of those who do wrong; for like the grass they will soon wither, like green plants they will soon die away. Trust in the Lord and do good; dwell in the land and enjoy safe pasture. Delight yourself in the Lord and he will give you the desires of your heart. Commit your way to the Lord; trust in him and he will do this: He will make your righteousness shine like the dawn, the justice of your cause like the noonday sun. Be still before the Lord and wait patiently for him…"

- Psalm 5:1–3: "Give ear to my words, O Lord, consider my sighing. Listen to my cry for help, my King and my God, for to you I pray. In the morning, O Lord, you hear my voice; in the morning I lay my requests before you and wait in expectation."

When you make a petition to God, wait for the answer. Be patient. Understand that in God's time, He will take care of your request. And if the request is handled in a way you don't expect or want, there's a reason for it. It could be to help make you more mature, more understanding, or more humble. It might even make you stop and realize who's in control. Wait on the Lord, and He will make it clear if it's important. If it doesn't become clear, you know that God loves you anyway. You know that God's in control. You know that Jesus has already won the battle. Wait for His answer.

Before we leave this thought, remember that Psalm 27:14 says, "Wait for the Lord; be strong and take heart and wait for the Lord."

BELIEVE IN GOD'S MIRACLES

The fourth way we can trust in the Lord is to believe in His miracles. Do miracles occur today? Do you believe in miracles? I do. I understand God can do miraculous things. We need to believe in prayer, miracles, and the power of God. After all, why pray to God if you don't think He can do things man can't?

I believe in the power of prayer, and I'll tell you why. When my grandson, Major, was born, he failed his hearing test. The doctors told us he had extensive nerve damage and a hearing impairment that could never be reversed. We were told the most we could hope for was that Major's condition would not get worse, but that it would certainly never get better. The experts said there was no medical evidence to support any chance for improvement. Before the little guy was even six months old, he was already wearing hearing aids. But through our family, church family, and friends' connections, people all across the U.S. began to pray for my grandson.

Major was tested by a therapist the other day. She was amazed to find his vocabulary is seven months ahead of his age group. He hasn't worn his hearing aids in almost two years. Our family has noticed on many occasions that Major is the first one to point out a noise in the background. He hears! Miracle? Touched by God? Answer to prayer? Yes, yes, and yes! Through prayer, our family has experienced firsthand the miracle of God's healing power.

It's time to believe in God's miracles and to thank Him for the way He touches our lives. I Chronicles 16:8–12 is a great place to start:

> Give thanks to the LORD, call on his name; make known among the nations what he has done. Sing to him, sing praise to him; tell of all his wonderful acts. Glory in his holy name; let the hearts of those who seek the LORD rejoice. Look to the LORD and his strength; seek his face always. Remember the wonders he has done, his miracles, and the judgments he pronounced.

REJOICE IN GOD'S GOODNESS

The fifth way to trust is to rejoice in God's goodness. In the Bible, David encountered many dangers and obstacles. He sinned at times and also made many enemies. When difficulties surrounded David, he knew he needed God's love, protection and goodness. As he wrote in Psalm 13:1–6:

How long, O Lord? Will you forget me forever? How long will you hide your face from me? How long must I wrestle with my thoughts and every day have sorrow in my heart? How long will my enemy triumph over me? Look on me and answer, O Lord my God. Give light to my eyes, or I will sleep in death; my enemy will say, "I have overcome him," and my foes will rejoice when I fall. But I trust in your unfailing love; my heart rejoices in your salvation. I will sing to the Lord, for he has been good to me.

David also expressed rejoicing. In Psalm 32:10–11, he wrote:

Many are the woes of the wicked, but the LORD's unfailing love surrounds the man who trusts in him. Rejoice in the LORD and be glad, you righteous; sing, all you who are upright in heart!

We need to rejoice in the goodness of the Lord, because without it, we'd be lost and hopeless. We wouldn't have a chance. His goodness gives us life.

I wonder sometimes if I rejoice enough. I don't think I do. I spend too much time thinking about how things could be and not enough time being happy with how things are. To rejoice means to be glad. So, what do I have to be glad about?

Well, I'm married to an amazing woman I don't deserve. I've been blessed with two children who serve the Lord and are happily married. Both are successful in business. I consider my children's spouses as my own children—they are special. I have, like every grandparent would say, the two most wonderful grandkids in the world. They are healthy, smart, and full of life and joy.

Even more important, I am a child of God! I John 3:1 says, "How great is the love the Father has lavished on us, that we should be called children of God!" And not only are we *called* children of God, but we *are* children of God!

Have you ever smiled as you spoke to children about their moms? Most of the time, children are delighted to tell you about their moms. They can't control themselves as they tell how special their mom is and how she takes care of them. They tell you what she did for them that day, starting with the hug she gave them when they got out of bed. They will tell you about playing games with her and how she reads to them. Maybe they will mention how they made cookies together and even had fun cleaning up the mess. They are happy. They rejoice in their mother.

When we put the shoe on the other foot, we as parents can hardly contain our joy over our children. When I get a new picture of Mary Alice or Major, I take it to the office. I want my coworkers to see how beautiful my grandkids are. I have to be careful not to be obnoxious.

We are children, too. Not of this world, but of God. The way I just mentioned nurtured children feel about their parents is the same way we should feel as children of God. I imagine the way I feel about my children and grandchildren might offer a glimpse into the way God feels about us. We should be full of joy as God's children, and we should rejoice in Him.

How sad is it to hear from parents who have lost the love of their children. How tragic to learn of a parent who has rejected his or her child. I was talking to an old friend of mine a while back. I asked about his mom, and he replied, "I haven't talked to her in several years." How sad. I know the reason. She had a tendency to drive a wedge between him and his wife. So, my friend felt it was necessary to separate his family from his mom. I agree that was a wise course of action, but it is still sad. There is something wrong with that family unit. It is sick because of the actions of one of its members. The same thing can happen to our relationship with God if we aren't watchful. A person or circumstance can drive a wedge between us and God. Suddenly, our relationship with God is strained and the joy we once shared is gone.

Don't let it happen. Don't allow life or people to rob you of the joy of belonging to God. Just as you would do anything in your power to protect your children or your parents, do everything you can to strengthen your relationship with God.

RELAX IN GOD'S PRESENCE

Finally, relax in God's presence. We talked about this in the first chapter when I encouraged you to be still and know that God is in control. Relax in His presence.

Psalm 116:1–9 talks about resting in the Lord because of His mighty works:

I love the LORD, for he heard my voice; he heard my cry for mercy. Because he turned his ear to me, I will call on him as long as I live. The cords of death entangled me, the anguish of the grave came upon me; I was overcome by trouble and sorrow. Then I called on the name of the LORD: "O LORD, save me!" The LORD is gracious and righteous; our God is full of compassion. The LORD protects the simple hearted; when I was in great need, he saved me. Be at rest once more, O my soul, for the LORD has been good to you. For you, O LORD, have delivered my soul from death, my eyes from tears, my feet from stumbling, that I may walk before the LORD in the land of the living.

How many times have you watched a baby fight off sleep? Isn't it funny to watch the struggle? The baby needs rest, but for some reason, he or she just won't relax. Why? The same question can be asked of us. Why do we refuse to relax and rest in the Lord? Why do we fight against what is good for us?

Now, what happens when a mother cuddles that baby? The touch of love, the comfort of an embrace, and the pleasure of security all bring about a feeling of safety. The baby who was struggling is now relaxed in his mother's arms as he gently falls asleep. He is peaceful and is being renewed in the comfort of his mother's touch.

You are that baby. It doesn't matter if you are one or ninety-seven; you are that baby. You are being touched by God, you are being embraced by the arms of the Creator, and you can relax and rest in the security of the Lord. Our heavenly Father would have us be still and know that He is God.

I hope the thoughts we've covered in this chapter have inspired and encouraged you to trust in the Lord more fully each day. Remember to trust, rely, wait, believe, rejoice, and relax. God bless you in your walk with Him.

One final note: Ken McLeroy passed away Wednesday, September 12, 2007. I was in Honduras assisting Wilson Howell and three other dentist doing teeth extractions when I received word of his death. We had only one more day of work planned and we would head back to Tegucigalpa on Friday morning, spend the night there, and then fly home on Saturday. I called Miranda and ask her to see if I could change my ticket and fly from Tegucigalpa to Lubbock on Friday. Dad would pick me up there and I would be able to meet up with Paula, Miranda and Josh who were driving in from Dallas for Ken's memorial service. Miranda told me that it could be done, but it would cost over five hundred dollars.

I counted the cost and knew that it was a price I would gladly pay. Service for those you love is priceless. I was able to keep my promise to Ken, and I stood and cried for fifteen or twenty minutes while celebrating with those in attendance, the life and service of Ken McLeroy.

THIRTEEN
WHEN PEACE LIKE A RIVER

One of my favorite songs is "When Peace Like a River" (you may also know it as "It Is Well with My Soul" written by Horatio G. Spafford). I started thinking about this topic because there have been so many times in my life when I didn't feel like I had peace. Where does peace fit in our lives, and just how do we obtain it?

I think we gain peace through a decision making process. We obtain peace because we strive for it. It doesn't just happen to us. Paul, as we talked about previously in Romans 7, didn't have true peace at the time he was writing that letter. He essentially says, "What I want to do, I don't do. What I shouldn't do, I continue doing." Paul struggled with conflicting spiritual and fleshly desires.

Let's look at Philippians 4:4–7:

> Rejoice in the LORD always. I will say it again: Rejoice! Let your gentleness be evident to all. The LORD is near. Do not be anxious about anything, but in everything, by prayer and petition, with thanksgiving, present your requests to God. And the peace of God, which transcends all understanding, will guard your hearts and your minds in Christ Jesus.

What does this passage of Scripture tell us to do? It tells us to lay everything at God's feet and present our requests to

Him. If we want peace, God will show us peace. And we're going to have to make a conscious effort to rejoice, even when we don't necessarily feel happy.

When I was growing up, some of my younger cousins would start crying for no reason. My uncle would tell them to stop, and if they didn't, he would make them stand in front of a mirror. It's nearly impossible to look at yourself in a mirror and cry, especially if you're crying for no reason. Pretty soon, you realize you look ridiculous. That's the way children are. They cry for no reason. We sometimes do the same thing as adults. We may be crying inside, moaning and groaning, and carrying on for no apparent reason. We have to make a choice not to moan and groan and rejoice instead.

This concept is hard for me, because I have a fuse as short as I am. I believe the Lord made me too slow to run and too small to fight for a reason: I've had to learn how to get along with folks. We have to learn to be gentle. Even large football players such as Merlin Olsen have a reputation for being gentle. He's a man who exhibits love through his life.

DON'T BE ANXIOUS

Don't be anxious about anything. I don't know about you, but I get anxious over some of the silliest things. When I managed a cotton gin, some of the members of the board of directors thought they were smarter than I was. Every now and then they questioned my decisions, so I never enjoyed board meetings. On board meeting days, I would wake up in a foul mood. Any time I was by myself, I played out the evening's likely discussion in my head, rehearsing my responses to the difficult questions I anticipated. I did that all day long so that by the time the board meeting came, I was bent out of shape; however, ninety-nine times out of one hundred, what I dreaded never happened. The conversations I fretted over in my mind never took place. I had made myself sick worrying for no reason. Why do we do that?

Maybe you've found yourself in a similar situation. If so, turn these circumstances over to God. You might be asking, "What do I turn over to God? Do I give God everything or just what I can't handle?" It's easy for me to admit I can't handle a 747, but maybe I can still handle a Piper Cub airplane. In reality, I need God's help when I'm flying a Piper Cub, too. I need God's help even when I'm doing the little things I'm good at because I can still make mistakes. Turn it all over to God. Give Him glory and honor by asking for His help.

You don't have peace if you're fighting with yourself all the time. It just doesn't happen. Colossians 3:15 says, "Let the peace of Christ rule in your hearts, since as members of one body you were called to peace. And be thankful."

We used a portion of this Scripture reference in one of our previous chapters, but Proverbs 3:5–18 ties in beautifully with the virtue of peace:

> Trust in the LORD with all your heart and lean not on your own understanding; in all your ways acknowledge him, and he will make your paths straight. Do not be wise in your own eyes; fear the

Lord and shun evil. This will bring health to your body and nourishment to your bones. Honor the Lord with your wealth, with the firstfruits of all your crops; then your barns will be filled to overflowing, and your vats will brim over with new wine. My son, do not despise the Lord's discipline and do not resent his rebuke, because the Lord disciplines those he loves, as a father the son he delights in. Blessed is the man who finds wisdom, the man who gains understanding, for she is more profitable than silver and yields better returns than gold. She is more precious than rubies; nothing you desire can compare with her. Long life is in her right hand; in her left hand are riches and honor. Her ways are pleasant ways, and all her paths are peace. She is a tree of life to those who embrace her; those who lay hold of her will be blessed.

This passage is talking about asking God for wisdom. But how do we seek and find wisdom? Once again, we have to understand that everything we do in our Christian lives is a decision. Initially, we may not want to do the things we know we should, but somewhere along the way we have to start wanting to do them. Willpower has to join us. We have to make a decision and follow through.

MAKE A DECISION

I understand addiction requires a tremendous amount of willpower (and God's help, of course) to overcome. How do you get away from nicotine or any other drug or behavior that has a grip on you? Again, it has to be a conscious decision. You have to make up your mind. Your spouse or kids can't make the decision for you. It has to be something *you* want to do.

My dad gave up smoking by walking in the house one day and throwing his pack of cigarettes on the table. We had a lazy susan in the middle of the table, and he put the cigarettes there. He told Mom, "I'm going to quit. But don't throw those things away." That open pack of cigarettes lay there for more than a year, but Dad never touched another one. Why? Because he made the decision on his own to quit. It wasn't Mom nagging him, and it wasn't his children asking him to stop. It was his decision.

So, if we're going to seek wisdom, offer up our lives to God and quit being anxious, we have to start with a decision. We don't attend Sunday morning worship just because we're supposed to be there (although I've been guilty of that on occasion). We make the decision to praise God, glorify the Father, and edify one another. In turn, we also benefit from fellowship that encourages us to continue making good decisions that bring us closer to Christ. These steps help bring us peace. Even when we find ourselves on a path with problems, if we focus on the will of God and ask for His help, peace begins ruling in our lives.

KEEP MOVING

Let's look at the first verse of the song "When Peace Like a River": "When peace like a river attendeth my way, when sorrows like sea billows roll. Whatever my lot, Thou hast taught me to say, 'It is well, it is well, with my soul.'" Now, if you're going to say it is well with your soul, you've got to have some peace, don't you?

Some friends of ours have a house in Ruidoso, New Mexico. It's a beautiful place. The best bedroom is in the back corner on the ground level because you can open the window at night and hear the nearby stream. You can listen to the wind blowing through the trees and the little stream as it trickles over the rocks. Talk about a way to forget your problems and start your prayers to God. Does the phrase "peace like a river" remind you of a similar special place? Maybe "peace like a river" reminds you of a peaceful mountain stream or even the lazy old Mississippi.

There are some things about a river that we need to know. Back when I was nineteen years old and spent six months in Blackfoot, Idaho, I went on a camping trip with the local church group. When we arrived at our site, the preacher told me, "You can drink out of the river where it's running over the rocks, because it's pure. You don't want to drink out of the river where it's a dead pool." I know what you're thinking, *Kent what about that dead elk lying up stream?* You are right it would not be wise to drink from that stream. However, my point is that a moving stream does not become stagnant; the movement keeps life-giving oxygen supplied to the stream.

As long as a river is moving at its intended pace, the water in that river is healthy. In the same way, when we're moving at the pace God intended us to move, our lives can be a peaceful river. But when we're trying to outrun God's pace, we're going to trip over some rocks. We could find ourselves in a class five rapid before we know it. And when we forget God altogether, we become that stale pool.

Why is the Dead Sea called the Dead Sea? The Jordan River brings water from the Sea of Galilee to the Dead Sea, but the water has no outlet from there, so it is dead. It's stagnant. Nothing can survive in the Dead Sea, and the salt content of the water is so high that it is dangerous to drink. When we stop moving in our Christian lives, we become dead and stagnant.   So, we have to keep moving. We have to continue our maturation process. As we grow in the love, knowledge, and wisdom of God and Jesus, our river keeps moving. There will be times when we encounter class five rapids in our lives. Sometimes these will be through no fault of our own, but other times they will be because we tried to handle things all by ourselves. Either way, we need to remember to reach out, take God's hand, and let Him lead us back to peaceful waters.

BELIEVE IN JESUS WHEN SEA BILLOWS ROLL

I'm reminded of a couple of accounts in Matthew when Jesus exhibits power to calm the water and wind. In Matthew 8, the disciples are all in the boat with Jesus as He is sleeping. When a storm develops, they wake Him, saying, "We're in danger! Lord, don't You care that we're about to drown?" Jesus replies, "Why are you scared?" Then He tells the winds and waves, "Peace. Be still."

All the disciples had to do was believe in Jesus and peace would be there. A few chapters later, in Matthew 14, Jesus walks on the water. Peter calls out to Jesus, saying,

"Lord, if it's You, let me come out to You." Jesus replies, "Okay. Come out to Me." As long as Peter looks at the Lord, he's walking on water. However, the moment he sees the winds and waves and becomes afraid, he begins to sink. But Jesus reaches out His hand to help him back into the boat. Then the winds subside.

Wouldn't that be a dream? I sometimes dream about flying without an airplane. Have you ever dreamed about walking on water? Think about it. All you have to do is look at Jesus. He's going to make your path straight.

The song "When Peace Like a River" contains the line, "When sorrows like sea billows roll." We all encounter sorrow in our lives. My family experienced sorrow when we found out my grandson, Major, had irreversible hearing problems. News like that tugs at you. And sea billows rolling? Yeah, there's a tendency for that. But you know what? When we look to Jesus, we find the silver lining in those difficult times. We need to look for the positives even when the sea is raging.

The song goes on to say, "Whatever my lot, Thou hast taught me to say, 'It is well with my soul.'" The apostle Paul said this as well when he wrote in Philippians 4:11, "...I have learned to be content whatever the circumstances." Now, that's a difficult attitude to maintain. Say you've been blessed with material possessions and a happy, healthy, and successful family. All of a sudden, you find yourself broke, you lose a child, and your spouse contracts cancer. What do you do? You have to learn to be content.

Another verse in the song says, "My sin, oh, the bliss of this glorious thought. My sin, not in part but the whole, is nailed to the cross, and I bear it no more, praise the Lord, praise the Lord, oh, my soul." Do we fully realize how much sin is present in our lives? If we don't, maybe we aren't able to completely appreciate the sacrifice that erased it. It's helpful to remember how much it cost Jesus to make that sacrifice. We have to make it personal by acknowledging it was our individual sins that put Him on the cross.

The responsibility is ours, just as Peter says in his sermon in Acts 2:22: "Men of Israel, listen to this: Jesus of Nazareth was a man accredited by God to you by miracles, wonders and signs..." He boldly goes on to tell them, "You nailed Him to the cross." And we did too! We can't deny responsibility for that, but we can turn it into the positive that God intended. It is a glorious thought that our sins—and not just the ones that are big, black and hairy, but also the ones that don't seem quite so bad—are covered. All sin is equal in God's book, and Jesus died for everyone because we all sin every day of our lives.

A few years ago, our Honduras mission team set up a big screen to show the film *The Passion of The Christ*. Many people there had never even seen a movie. Can you imagine the impact? It was phenomenal. People who had absolutely nothing compared to even the very least of us in the United States saw what Christ's sacrifice meant, and it became personal to them. Sometimes, I don't think we celebrate that fact enough. When we take the Lord's Supper, it should be a thought-provoking remembrance. When we commemorate that serious event, it is like the death of a loved one who dies in the Lord. We may cry at the funeral, but our hearts can sing because we know that person has overcome death and won the victory through Jesus.

KNOW WHERE YOU'RE GOING

The last verse of our song says, "And Lord, haste the day when the faith shall be sight, the clouds be rolled back as a scroll, the trump shall resound and the Lord shall descend, even so, it is well, with my soul." How many times have you sung that song but not really meant it?

When you have ultimate peace, you can sing that last verse and mean it. That's when you can sing with total conviction. Faith is the evidence of things hoped for (see Hebrews 11:1). We hope even though we haven't seen. When we see Jesus descending to the earth from heaven, we will see our faith realized. Yet we can't ask the Lord to hasten the day if we don't have peace. We can't honestly do that if we don't know which direction we're going when it's all over.

I have some Christian brothers and sisters who have no concept of grace. Rather than embracing the idea of walking in the light, they choose to live in fear every day that they might sin without knowing it and die before they're able to ask for forgiveness. They don't realize they have eternal life. To them, it's a gamble whether they will make it to heaven or not. They picture themselves standing before the judgment seat, scared to death and quivering like King Belshazzar when he saw the handwriting on the wall. Daniel 5:6 says, "His face turned pale and he was so frightened that his knees knocked together and his legs gave way."

You know what, folks? I believe it's going to be awesome when we stand before the judgment seat, but I don't believe we're going to stand there with quivering knees and frightened faces. I don't think we're going to be scared to death. We will know where we are going. We should know that now, because we have the promise now. All we have to do is receive it. All we have to do is live in peace.

Part of me isn't ready for the Lord to return yet, because I want to see my grandchildren grow up. Nothing makes my day like receiving a new photo of my grandkids. There are other people and things I want to hold onto here. And, praise God, my family's been blessed to see my grandson, Major, healed from his hearing impairment. I've told you about that. But as Christians, we need to realize there's something beyond what's here and now. We need to adjust our mindsets from the self-centered approach that says this world is as good as it gets. It's easy to get so wrapped up in our current enjoyment that we forget what even greater blessings await us on the other side.

Make today a glorious day for yourself, your family, your friends, your Christian brothers and sisters and, most of all, your God. Even though you will experience problems on this earth, it's a wonderful life, isn't it? Talk about chill bumps. When you think about the clouds rolling back as a scroll and the Lord descending—that's going to be a great day. If you're living at peace now—if you have peace like a river in your heart—you can honestly say you're looking forward to that day. You can honestly say, "Lord, come quickly."

It is well with my soul.

Please go to, www.grumpysmith.com for information on Kent's future projects, speaking engagements and to listen to excerpts from the original series taught at the Church of Christ on McDermott Road. Kent is available to present lessons for seminars, retreats, gospel meetings/ revivals, or Sunday sermons. A student study guide has been written by Mike Willoughby and can be ordered along with more copies of Everyday Christianity.

Check the web site for updates on the release of Grumpy Smith's next book:

Completely Eat Up by a Case of the Stupids